The ultimate **Fairies** handbook

DEDICATION

To MY PARENTS ♥ ♥ ♥

To my mother and father,
for introducing me to the piskies and stones,
and to my girls, for living in fairyland.

The ultimate **Fairies** handbook

SUSANNAH MARRIOTT

MQP

	Introduction	6
chapter 1	Fairy Realms	8
chapter 2	Anatomy of a Fairy	64
chapter 3	A Fairy's Day	108
chapter 4	Helpful Spirits	152
chapter 5	Mischievous Work	192
chapter 6	Powers of Enchantment	236
chapter 7	Fairies on the Margins	286
chapter 8	Fairy Trees and Flowers	328
chapter 9	Meeting the Fay	370
	Bibliography	416
	Picture Credits	416
	Index	426

Introduction

Fairies have attached themselves to me for the past 40 years. I was brought up by my Cornish mother to break my egg shells, should a little person want to fly in them, and to honor the piskies in case they got angry. My father marched us around standing stones, taught us to trace ley lines, and passed on country lore he'd learnt from his blacksmith father, who brewed healing potions from hedgerow herbs. At university I wrote a thesis on nineteenth-century fairy painting, and my first job found me working for the UK Brownies organization. This was set up for girls aged between seven and ten, and was inspired by the example of the ever-helpful house pixies called Brownies.

But it wasn't until my own children came along that the wee folk really started to come into their own, and I find myself passing on, in turn, all the fairy lore I have amassed, and more. As a parent you have the privilege of becoming those shady nighttime figures, the tooth fairy, and the "jolly old elf" Santa Claus, and of fixing the Christmas fairy to the top of the tree. I now have every excuse for lying in long grass looking for fairies, for following piskie trails through the woods, and for visiting again the many sites near our home in Cornwall with fairy connections.

Just as fairy lore is a mish-mash of beliefs, stitched into each other like patchwork, and cut and pasted into a crazy-quilt, so this book is my collected album of thoughts on fairies. It jumps from traditional tales to noting places where the fair ones have settled today: and to news of gnome liberation groups. You will notice that many of the tales told within these pages sit at odds with their images, for the perception of fairies has fixed differently in word and image. Tales coagulated around mischief, danger, and respect; images around the delight of tiny creatures, perfect in every detail, and on truthful representations of nature. Fairies have always been seen as archaic, but I believe they have something to say to us in the twenty-first century; they keep open the promise that no matter where we live and whatever life we seem stuck in, another world exists, where everything is possible, if only we believe enough. Grab a four-leaf clover and prepare to be transported.

Susannah Marriott
Cornwall 2006

previous page 2: **Illustration from *Elfin Song,* Florence Harrison, 1912, British**
previous page 4: **Illustration from *Elfin Song,* Florence Harrison, 1912, British**

chapter 1
Fairy Realms

Enter these enchanted woods,
You who dare.
Nothing harms beneath the leaves,
More than waves a swimmer cleaves.
Toss your heart up with the lark,
Foot at peace with mouse and worm,
Fair you fare.
Only at a dread of dark
Quaver, and they quit their form:
Thousand eyeballs under hoods
Have you by the hair.
Enter those enchanted woods
You who dare.

GEORGE MEREDITH, *THE WOODS OF WESTERMAIN*

previous page: **The Fairy Queen Takes an Airy Drive in a Light Carriage,
Richard Doyle, *In Fairyland,* 1870, British**
A delicate watercolor vision of her fairy majesty in flight.
right: **From *Elfin Song,* Florence Harrison, 1912, British**
Inviting fairies play golden pipes and entice a child into the wood.

Fairies of the forest

As far back as the sixteenth century, the philosopher Paracelsus defined the elemental spirits of nature. Those who were guardians of trees and other vegetation he described as dryads. Such fairies live not in a far-off land beyond the mountains, but on the edges of the human world, just beyond the boundary fence and village border. They guard their woodland wilderness jealously from those who dare to venture within. There are countless tales of a lone traveler lost in the woods as night approaches—darkness magnifies fear and the loss of the familiar— becoming ever more tangled, confused, and perhaps even a little thrilled as he or she draws away from the mores and taste of the civilized world. For the boundaries of cleared, settled land are also boundaries between what is known and permissible and what remains temptingly other.

The tangle of the unknown awaits those who have to leave the safety of the settlement: travelers and hunters, women leaving one village to marry in another. Especially at risk, from Russia to Ghana, are young beautiful girls. But in the forest one can also retreat from society and find nurturing shelter. Since it is a place where meetings are possible between two worlds, the forest is full of possibilities for self-transformation and spiritual empowerment. In Central America, mortals who heed the lessons of forest fairies can become shaman, for spirits of the forest have dominion over its plants, birds, and beasts.

right: **Kilmeny, Warwick Goble from *The Book of Fairy Poetry,* 1920, British**
The maid Kilmeny was fatally enchanted by fairy spirits of the forest.

Hunting trophies or spiritual powers may be offered up to those who are worthy, or who make appropriate offerings: prayers or pancakes, wine or incantations, tobacco or the first animal bagged. Though scary, the forest is, for those who live on its margins, the great provider, source of hearth and home, in the form of building materials, firewood, and fish or fowl to cook over that fire.

When the Lyeshy goes round to inspect his domains, the forest roars around him and the trees shake. By night he sleeps in some hut in the depths of the woods, and if by chance he finds that a belated traveler or sportsman has taken up his quarters in the refuge he had intended for himself, he strives hard to turn out the intruder, sweeping over the hut in the form of a whirlwind which makes the door rattle and the roof heave, while all around the trees bend and writhe, and a terrible howling goes through the forest. If, in spite of all these hints, the uninvited guest will not retire, he runs the risk of being lost next day in the woods, or swallowed up in a swamp.

W. R. S. RALSTON, *SONGS OF THE RUSSIAN PEOPLE*

left: **Puck seated on a spider's thread, Warwick Goble from *The Book of Fairy Poetry,* 1920, British**
Wander in the woods and you might stumble upon this laughing sprite.

Enticing elves

Mischievous spirits take pleasure in deluding travelers who step into their territory. They might remove or turn signs, or adopt more magical means to urge mortals to venture beyond the civilized space and deeper into the unknown. Able to shape-shift between animal, vegetable, and mineral as they move through the vegetation, fairies might manifest as a familiar tree, a fellow traveler with useful directions, or as an alluring sound.

Maybe the call is of a friend in distress (a trick of West Malaysia's *Orang Bunyi,* or voice people), or mysterious musical tones. Zaire's *Eloko,* human-devouring dwarves, use tinkling bells, which can be heard for miles trembling in the air, distorting man's senses and sense. For other woodland spirits seduction is a temptation mortals cannot resist. In Greek mythology, woodland was the dominion of the deity Pan, ruler of lustful pursuit and unwanted advances that lead humans to the state of alarm named after him — "panic."

The sexual charge of the forest motivates many of its denizens. Sweden's wood-caretaker *Skogsrå,* or woman of the forest, may materialize as a tiny, fabulously beautiful woman, most elegantly dressed or exquisitely naked but for her long, auburn locks. She approaches hunters, charcoal burners, or other woodsmen, beckoning them away from the safety of the campfire. Once smitten, they are ever at her beck and call, enticed into trysts deep in the forest after dark. Thus entrapped, young men lose more than their way; they may lose their minds, able only to bleat like a calf. But though she is tricky and disruptive, a respectful dalliance with a *Skogsrå* may be worth a gamble, even today, since she can reward with good hunting if well pleased by tributes. Other forest spirits live a give-and-take life on the edge of our world, drawn into human habitation for food and other sustenance, physical or emotional. German *Holz-frauen,* Wood-wives, similar to the *Skogsrå*, are enticed by the scent of baking bread, and may turn up in a kitchen to borrow something, or ask in the woods for a barrow to be mended. To give of time and skills willingly is to be rewarded with wood chips, which may turn to gold.

previous page: **Asleep in the Moonlight, Richard Doyle from *In Fairyland,* 1870, British**
above: **Elves playing, Warwick Goble from *The Book of Fairy Poetry,* 1920, British**

Water sprites

Worlds beneath the waves seem fitting places for fairy folk, since they are dwellings that enchant mortals, but in which we cannot linger for long. In order to stay we must sacrifice life in the human world: water divides the living from the dead in many traditions. Since water is a female-linked element, and many of the creatures in its realm are associated with fertility and fickleness, it is not surprising that it is a sexual undertow that drags people into these realms. It is fatal, however, for while alive we cannot enjoy the company of the mer and their watery cousins; we have to slough off our skins to join them.

Half-birds, half-women, classical sirens or sea nymphs patrolled rocky outcrops like territorial seagulls. They did not squawk, but sang so melodiously they lured all within earshot to their doom. The Mermaid, half-fish, half-woman, like Sweden's *Sjörå*, entices with her unearthly beauty, wrecking boats and the men who work them. Those captivated are grasped to death in eager arms, or, in Portuguese tales, they are eaten. Other stories have mer-men capture the souls of lost mortals beneath overturned lobster pots fathoms below the ocean surface. In Russia, the *Rusalka* tickles her male prey to death with playful eroticism. The rivers and ponds of Germany are attended by *Nixies*, freshwater fish women intent on luring men to their ruin. Better not cross one of these by saving a drowning soul; she demands a yearly sacrifice as her dues.

left: **A fairy by the sea, Warwick Goble from *The Book of Fairy Poetry*, 1920, British**
The shoreline is a known haunt of enchanting water sprites.

My palace is in the coral cave
Set with spars by the ocean wave;
Would ye have gems, then seek them there,
There found I the pearls that bind my hair.
I and the wind together can roam
Over the green waves and their white foam,
See, I have got this silver shell,
Mark how my breath will its smallness swell,
For the Nautilus is my boat
In which I over the waters float,
The moon is shining over the sea,
Who is there will come sail with me?

L.E LANDON, *FAIRIES ON THE SEA-SHORE*

right: **A fairy riding a nautilus, Warwick Goble from *The Book of Fairy Poetry,* 1920, British**

Tiny sea fairies use discarded shells aa a graceful mode of transport.

A mermaid

Who would be
A mermaid fair,
Singing alone,
Combing her hair
Under the sea,
In a golden curl
With a comb of pearl,
On a throne?

I would be a mermaid fair;
I would sing to myself the whole of the day;
With a comb of pearl I would comb my hair;
And still as I comb'd I would sing and say,
'Who is it loves me? who loves not me?'

left: **A mermaid combing her hair, Warwick Goble from *The Book of Fairy Poetry,* 1920, British**

Mermaids are renowned for their incredible beauty; they constantly tend their seductive, flowing locks, while luring helpless mortals to their doom.

I would comb my hair till my ringlets would fall
        Low adown, low adown,
From under my starry sea-bud crown
        Low adown and around,
And I should look like a fountain of gold
    Springing alone
    With a shrill inner sound
        Over the throne
    In the midst of the hall;

Till that great sea-snake under the sea
From his coiled sleeps in the central deeps
Would slowly trail himself sevenfold
Round the hall where I sate, and look in at the gate
With his large calm eyes for the love of me.
And all the mermen under the sea
Would feel their immortality
Die in their hearts for the love of me.

ALFRED, LORD TENNYSON, *A MERMAID*

above: **The Sea-Fairies**, Warwick Goble from *The Book of Fairy Poetry*, 1920, British

Fish out of water

Mortals transported to glittery underwater palaces fail to thrive, even if they do escape, but a surprising number of fairy folk can survive away from their watery realm, albeit with great sadness and longing for home. The Shetland Selkie, or seal woman, abandons her half-human children, though she loves them dearly, to return to the sea once she has found her hidden seal skin. In contrast, the Russian *Rusalka* sustains herself on land with a magical comb that, as she pulls it through her hair, brings her waves of restorative moisture.

This siren comes ashore in spring, to hang out on boughs, enticing all comers on moonlit nights with her alluring laugh and song, or dancing with blazing eyes, playfully moving loose, wet, green, wavy locks over her snow-white breasts. Mortals fête her in a week-long spring festival called *Rusal'naia nedelia,* when she dances moisture over the crops: you know it's her by the sound of splashing water as women circle-dance over the fields in her honor, offering dyed eggs, blini, and garlands for her hair.

And yet, mortal women also fear her power; part of the celebrations includes forming a body from a birch tree, singing erotic songs for the *Rusalka* doll, then drowning her in the river, just as she drowns those she takes as her lovers.

right: **Sea nymphs, Warwick Goble from *The Book of Fairy Poetry,* 1920, British**
Sea fairies play in their natural element—a dangerous place for mortals .

WARWICK GOBLE

Come, dear children, let us away;
Down and away below!
Now my brothers call from the bay,
Now the great winds shoreward blow,
Now the salt tides seaward flow;
Now the wild white horses play,
Champ and chafe and toss in the spray.
Children dear, let us away!
This way, this way!

Call her once before you go—
Call once yet!
In a voice that she will know:
"Margaret! Margaret!"
Children's voices should be dear
(Call once more) to a mother's ear;
Children's voices, wild with pain—
Surely she will come again!
Call her once and come away;
This way, this way!
"Mother dear, we cannot stay!
The wild white horses foam and fret."
Margaret! Margaret!

Come, dear children, come away down;
Call no more!
One last look at the white-walled town,
And the little grey church on the windy shore;
Then come down!
She will not come though you call all day;
Come away, come away!

MATTHEW ARNOLD, *THE FORSAKEN MERMAN*

Air fairies

Some spirits of the air take charge of clouds, wind, and storms. Native American Cloud People use these gifts kindly to bring about renewing rainfall, like the tiny Cantabrian wind spirits of northern Spain, the *Ventolines*, or "little winds," who guide fishing craft safely into harbor. Others have more destructive intent. Slavonia's *Vily* inhabits violent windstorms, like the *Skogsrå* of Swedish forests. Some of the Valkyries, battle nymphs of Nordic and Teutonic lore, fly on clouds above the action with names like *Mist* (meaning cloud grey), *Hrist* (storm), and *Wolkenthrut* (cloud power).

Japan's *Yuki-Onna,* or snow maiden, may appear as a hovering mist of white vapor, in which form she penetrates the home, bringing the dangers of the wilderness into the heart of civilization. Incredibly, ethereally, palely beautiful in frost-white robes (in which form she may marry mortals), she creeps through unguarded windows and doors in the form of a mist, inhaling human life-force in a reverse kiss of life, or enticing men out into her domain, the blizzard, to perish. In Italy, the *Folletti*, wind knot fairies stir up tiny dust storms to carry them through the keyhole.

previous page: **Illustration from *Elfin Song,* Florence Harrison, 1912, British**
left: **The North Wind Fairy, Florence Harrison, from *Elfin Song,* 1912, British**
This wind-borne fairy flies in a white fury, bringing snow and ice with her.

Ljósálfar, the light *Alfs* of Norse mythology, live in the sky in *Álfheim*, a luminous heavenly mansion that sits at the highest level of the Norse nine worlds, though little is written or told of the place. Clouds are often associated with divine realms: in the *Qur'an* and the Bible God offers guidance from a cloud; in China they stand for mortal ascent to the heavens. Cloud may even be the stuff of fairy bodies. In the seventeenth century, Scottish minister Robert Kirk wrote in one of the definitive works on fairy lore that the wee folk are formed from "congealed Air" or "condensed cloud." The philosopher Paracelsus maintained that the elements air and wind are embodied in sylphs, described as very tall and strong, with a personality corresponding to their power over tempests and storms. Such air spirits are often represented with wings, as quick-moving, transparent, or glowing, and seen only at the periphery of human vision.

Other air-bound fairies materialize as a flickering phosphorescence hovering above lonely ground, or making their way like a band of invisible travelers with lamps over a twisting, turning hillside. Such spirits inhabit another nefarious zone on the edge of human settlement: marshland and hillside. Is this Will o' the *Wisp*—*Lyktgubbe* in Sweden, *Sand Yan y Tad* in Brittany—the life-force made visible, of spirits lost in marshland and rivers, or, as scientific sources say, the spontaneous ignition of vegetable matter?

Such elf fire might lead late-night trespassers to safety, but more often as not it takes them further into the spirit's boggy domain: the mist might lift to find the trusting traveler standing atop a precipice, the foaming sea booming far far below.

These siths or Fairies … are said to be of a middle nature betwixt man and Angel, as were daemons thought to be of old: of intelligent Studious Spirits, and light changeable bodies, like those called Astral, somewhat of the nature of a condensed cloud, and best seen in twilight. These bodies are so pliable through the subtlety of the spirits that agitate them, that they can make them appear or disappear at pleasure.

ROBERT KIRK, *THE SECRET COMMONWEALTH OF ELVES, FAUNS AND FAIRIES*

Fairies of the earth

Scandinavian lore describes legions of human-shaped tiny folk who live beneath the earth; in Norway these *Underjordiske* are the most numerous of the *Hulderfolk*, the hidden people. They live within ancient burial mounds and mountains. In many cultures, mountains represent a place where the human world and the heavens meet. In 2006 there was a plea for people to stop scattering the ashes of loved ones on the summits of Scottish mountains: the practice has become so widespread that it is transforming the pH of the soil. Mountains are also the source of precious minerals and stones, so it is not surprising that fairy caverns and underground palaces are treasure-filled.

Subterranean folk gather in underground palaces. In Celtic areas these have long been associated with barrows, hill forts, and stone monuments (Breton tales tell of elf villages amid "rows of towering stones.") Irish fairy forts are said to be the mounds to which the island's original inhabitants, the *Tuatha dé Danaan*, fled when they lost their land to invaders. Fairy legends attach to many circular earth enclosures, or ring forts, known as *sidh* or *rath* in Ireland, and *knowes* in Scotland. Several thousand exist, many untouched by the farmers whose land they lie on: one moves a stone or harms a tree on a fairy *rath* at one's peril. Witnesses describe seeing hundreds of tiny lights stream from them after dusk, or catching a myriad tiny figures dressed for revels dancing within the enclosure banks to fiddle tunes or silver pipes.

right: Underground realms, Warwick Goble from *The Book of Fairy Poetry*, 1920, British
A glittering fairy hovers at the entrance to a secret underground dwelling.

Underground palaces

Tales that take us inside a fairy *rath* describe crystal halls lit by diamonds and lined with dazzling ornament. They tell of magnificent suppers with wine redder than rubies served by crowds of servants in expensive liveries. Fairies are passionate about pageant and go in for outrageous bling. Always there is music, dancing, and raucous merriment, for as a Welsh midwife told folk tale collector John Rhys, she had never spent any part of her life so merrily, "for there naught but festivity went on day and night: dancing, singing, and endless rejoicing reigned there." Sometimes those spirited away enter impressive country houses, attended by gorgeous servants attired in costly suits of brightly colored velvet. Again, there are grand ballrooms and dining halls, and tables groaning with good food.

But all is illusion. Like the fairy *rath* that, during the daylight is made of mere clods of earth, these palaces are never all they seem. Many stories tell of visitors' eyes being touched by fairy ointment, which reveals the reality behind the enchantment. Then they see through the artifice to another plane. That vision can be horrifiying.

They might be in a "frightful" musty cave, so dark you cannot see your hand before your face. In one tale the eye-witness states, "The beautiful room was a big rough cave, with water oozing over the edges of the stones and through the clay. And the lady, and the lord, and the child, wizened, poverty-bitten creatures—nothing but skin and bone, and the rich dresses were old rags."

He was no sooner in than he found himself in a palace glittering with gold and pearls. Every form of beauty surrounded him, and every variety of pleasure was offered him. He was made free to range whither he would, and his every movement was waited on by young women of the most matchless loveliness. And no tongue can tell the joys of feasting that were his. Instead of the tatws-a-llaeth (potatoes and butter-milk) to which he had hitherto been accustomed, here were birds and meats of every choice description, served on plates of silver. Instead of home-brewed *cwrw*, the only bacchic beverage he had ever tasted in real life, here were red and yellow wines of wondrous enjoyableness, brought in golden goblets richly inlaid with gems. The waiters were the most beautiful virgins, and everything was in abundance.

WIRT SIKES, *BRITISH GOBLINS: WELSH FOLK-LORE, FAIRY MYTHOLOGY, LEGENDS AND TRADITIONS*

Miniature miners

In Teutonic myth, dwarves are spirits of the earth who live in their thousands in cavernous cities mined underground or forged into the clefts of cliffs. So low at the entrance are these hidden caves that a man has to crawl to enter inside. Expert miners and tunnelers, dwarves industriously construct cavern after cavern, creating not only great halls, but fine grottoes and labyrinthine complexes of side passages. The Grimm brothers describe door after door, each opening to a little room, where dwarves can store the exquisite treasures they make: magically charged jewels and weapons forged from base metal. They are renowned for gathering and hoarding their treasures—and guarding them fiercely:

The dwarves of yore made mighty spells, While hammers fell like ringing bells …

J.R. TOLKIEN, *THE HOBBIT*

left: **A procession of gnomes, Warwick Goble from *The Book of Fairy Poetry,* 1920, British**
Gnomes stride out with a purposeful demeanor—all set to go to work.

How to find fairy lairs

Here is a little field guide to spotting fairy raths. These are important areas of ecology: because of the taboos surrounding them, they have largely been left untouched on farmland, so look for unusual flora and fauna. Take nothing away, and leave no trace of your visit. Look for:

Hill or mound: even a small hillock might be the haunt of fairies. They are usually circular. Welsh elves are said to haunt "dingles" or hollows by the wayside.

Wooded site: look for mature, indigenous, broadleaf trees, often in a circular cluster. In Scotland you might spot Scots pines.

Archeological features: on a map, look for nearby barrows and tumuli.In particular look for burial sites: in Celtic mythology underground fairy worlds are associated with the underworld.

Visually distinct: fairy sites tend to stand out from their surroundings. In farmland they will look wild, because of the taboo on their cultivation for generations.

Boundary site: often these sites mark a boundary between different communities, and may be some distance from human habitation. Because people both feared and venerated these sites, they avoided building homes and roads on or near them.

Legend and lore: look for place names associated with fairies or mythical beasts and ask about local superstitions.

right: **A Fairy Caravan, Charles Robinson from _The Children's Wonder Book,_ 1933, British**
You might be lucky enough to find fairies at the bottom of your garden.

Portals to fairy worlds

Though we are made of different stuff from them, fairies are able to cross into our world, and we can be transported to their Land of Promise, as it is spoken of in some sources. The Irish poet W. B. Yeats imagined this crossing over as a magnetic pushing-pulling attraction one for the other. We need the fairy world because it represents everything that is possible beyond our routine life and offers transformation and enlightening creativity. They need us to bring them to life. But the two can never fuse: we are as unalike as day and night, and, like day and night, we define each other.

For those brave enough to seek them out, there are doorways to these other worlds. Sometimes they are stumbled upon. They might be opened up to admit entry to those the fairies need: fiddlers and midwives are good examples. In modern fairy stories, it is the child who reaches the other world; for children have the ability to suspend disbelief at a given moment, pick up signs that something is not quite right, and have the curiosity and bravery to walk through. Fairyland is all around, waiting for us to find a way in claims the pioneering science writer Mrs Buckley, who in 1879 sought to introduce to children seemingly impossible forces of nature by picturing each as a fairy.

previous page: **Fairies' Wood by Thomas Bromley Blacklock, 1903, Scottish, (Kirkcudbright School)**
Fairies like to hide in secluded woodland settings.
right: **Florence Harrison, from *Elfin Song*, 1912, British**
Children are more easily alert to fairy presences.

There are many examples of people finding their way into the fairy world. For instance, in Welsh tales a farmer might find a door in a rock by a fairy lake. Given sufficient curiosity and resolution, he opens it, and is conducted along a secret passage to a fairy land. In America, the Iroquois summon little spirits by knocking on a decreed large stone. And there are even more tried and tested methods: German legend has it that touching a primrose, or number of primroses, on a floral fairy door opens the route to a fairy castle. Some report seeing a door ajar in hilltop earthworks or stone tombs, perhaps seeing fairy folk dressed for a celebration in the candlelit interior. The figure of British legend Child Rowland enters Elfland on a quest to save his sister by circling a green terraced mound three times widershins, against the turning of the sun, repeating each time the words

> "Open, door! open, door!
> And let me come in."

Scottish fairies cry "Hose and Hattock" to get home. Echo the call and you, too, might be teleported.

next page: **The Dance of the Little People, William Holmes Sullivan, c. 1890–1908, British**
Fairies cannot resist the lure of music, and may be tempted out of hiding by an expert piper or fiddle player.

There are *forces* around us, and among us, which I shall ask you to allow me to call *fairies*, and these are ten thousand times more wonderful, more magical, and more beautiful in their work, than those of the old fairy tales. … Just go out into the country, and sit down quietly and watch nature at work. Listen to the wind as it blows, look at the clouds rolling overhead, and waves rippling on the pond at your feet. Hearken to the brook as it flows by, watch the flower-buds opening one by one, and then ask yourself, "How all this is done?" Go out in the evening and see the dew gather drop by drop upon the grass, or trace the delicate hoar-frost crystals which bespangle every blade on a winter's morning. Look at the vivid flashes of lightning in a storm, and listen to the pealing thunder: and then tell me, by what machinery is all this wonderful work done? Man does none of it, neither could he stop it if he were to try; for it is all the work of those invisible *forces* or *fairies* whose acquaintance I wish you to make. Day and night, summer and winter, storm or calm, these fairies are at work, and we may hear them and know them, and make friends of them if we will.

ARABELLA B. BUCKLEY, *THE FAIRY-LAND OF SCIENCE*

Step into the ring

A sure way to enter the land of the little folk is by venturing to a fairy mound after dusk or stepping into a fairy ring. Another circular entrance is provided by a hag stone—this is a rock that has been hollowed by running water: simply look through it to catch a glimpse of fairyland. Listening to fairy tunes is similarly mind-altering, freeing the brain from temporal and mental constraints.

Another way is by becoming absorbed in looking at fairy painting and illustration. The painterly skill and detail of many nineteenth-century fairy images causes the brain to fizz, as if under a fairy spell—look at the hordes of tiny, perfect figures in Joseph Noel Paton's *Oberon and Titania Reconciled*, shown on pages 112–113. Hundreds of details engage your attention. The ordinariness of the impossible, and the otherness in a truthful depiction of nature, entrances the brain—dazzled by fairy dust. Gaze at Edward Robert Hughes' *Midsummer Eve* (opposite) and let yourself be drawn under the spell that the painter evokes.

left: Midsummer Eve, Edward Robert Hughes, 1908, British
This world-famous fairy painting depicts the magic and mystery of the most propitious night in the year for seeing fairies.

Crossover worlds

Through the entry door to the world of fairy, one might see both worlds juxtaposed, aware of the sounds, scents, and sights of the "real" world disconcertingly unchanged as a veil lifts on another scene. In *The Enchanted Cave of Cesh Corran,* James Stephens relates how the great chief Fionn mac Uail, out hunting with Cona'n the Swearer moves into the faery realm, though yet in the "real" world of the hunt.

"Fionn looked up at the sky and found that it was still there. He stared to one side and saw the trees of Kyle Conor waving in the distance. He bent his ear to the wind and heard the shouting of hunters, the yapping of dogs, and the clear whistles, which told how the hunt was going.

"Well!" said Fionn to himself.

"By my hand!" quoth Cona'n to his own soul.

And the two men stared into the hillside as though what they were looking at was too wonderful to be looked away from.

"Who are they?" said Fionn.

"What are they?" Cona'n gasped. And they stared again.

For there was a great hole like a doorway in the side of the mound, and in that doorway the daughters of Conaran sat spinning. They had three crooked sticks of holly set up before the cave, and they were reeling yarn off these. But it was enchantment they were weaving."

right: Lantern slide from the series *Gossip about Fairies,* 19th century
Moonlit fairies inhabit a parallel world just a glance away.

The entrance fee

For those admitted beyond the velvet rope there is often a price, since the laws of physics do not apply in fairyland. Some mortals spend a lifetime away, yet reappear in their ordinary lives at the moment they disappeared. Others only blink in fairyland, yet return "home" to find everyone grown and gone. They must hunt in vain for a way to return to the faery, for they no longer have a place on earth. Mortal lovers of the lake-dwelling Rusalka turn to dust on re-entry; and a Welsh tale ends abruptly thus, "Then he stepped from the fairy circle and instantly crumbled away and mingled his dust with the earth." Similar tales are told in Indian cities, of people who disappeared only last week.

STORY EXTRACT

The reluctant godparent

"A poor but pious servant girl … was busy cleaning out the house. Just as she about to carry the sweepings outside, she discovered a letter lying in her dustpan. It was addressed to her. Standing her broom against the wall, she read it. In the letter she was summoned to stand in as a godparent for a dwarf child the next day, and was promised that no harm would come to her.

She did not want to do this, but her employers told her that she must not decline, for if she did so, it would not go well for her. Thus she went forth that night, for that was when she was told to come. At twelve o'clock the mountain opened …

… After giving the child a name, they laid it into a golden cradle, and the musicians played until it fell asleep again. Then they had the best things to eat and drink, after which they danced and sang until morning on a large meadow. After they were tired, the girl said that she wanted to return home, but the dwarves begged and begged until she finally agreed to stay three more days, and all three days were filled with pleasure and joy.

When she finally started out for home, the dwarves rewarded her most generously and told her that the golden cradle would be saved for her forever. Then they opened the mountain and let her go.

The servant girl went home and took the broom from the wall in order to sweep out the entranceway. But behold, the house had changed completely during the three days. The entranceway was completely different. The cows had a different sound and a different color, and her good old white horse was gone. Some people approached her, but she did not know any of them. They spoke differently and wore different clothing

And no one knew anything about her. She told them all about her employers, but no one remembered them. And they all stared at her.

Now in Gilde there lived an old shepherd who himself did not know how old he was, and no one else knew it either. When he heard about the girl, he came over and said that his grandfather had told him that when his father was young, a girl had gone to the dwarves and had not returned.

That instant the girl turned into an ancient woman, collapsed, and was dead."

CARL AND THEODOR COLSHORN, *THE DWARVES IN SCHALK MOUNTAIN*

Fairy places to visit

Tomnahurich Hill, Inverness, Scotland: a famed tree-covered fairy hill, where mortal fiddlers have been lured to play for fairy folk.

Erdmannshöhle (Dwarf Cave), Hasel, near Schopfheim, Germany: scene of many dwarf legends and now a show cavern on two levels.

Troldhaugen (Troll's Hill), Paradis-Bergen, Norway: the home of the composer Grieg is now a museum. Visit the hut where he composed.

Trollkyrka (Troll's Church mountain), Tiveden, Sweden: the scene of well documented historical fairy rites. Follow a trail up the "tower."

Beal Boru ring fort, Killaloe, County Clare, Ireland: Brian Boru's fort overlooking a lough; he is the only person ever to ride the Pooka.

Lough Gur, County Limerick, Ireland: 5,000 year-old settlement with cave said to be an entrance to Tir na nOg, land of eternal youth.

Vysoka, Pribram, Czech Republic: composer Dvorak's country house and the source of his fairy inspiration, Rusalka lake.

Brocéliande (Forêt de Paimpont), Brittany, France: Merlin's forest of Arthurian legend and the haunt of forest fairies. Seek out the Fountain of Eternal Youth, near Barenton.

European gnome sanctuary, Barga, Lucca, Italy: a wooded valley is the first home of its kind for liberated spirits.

Fairies Tree, Fitzroy Gardens, Melbourne, Australia: place of pilgrimage for children to leave fairy letters and gifts.

Kensington Gardens, London: Read J.M. Barrie's *Peter Pan in Kensington Gardens* for his enthralling account of a favorite fairy haunt.

right: From *Peter Pan in Kensington Gardens,* Arthur Rackham, 1906
Visit London's Serpentine lake—a renowned fairy location.

The land of fairy, where nobody gets old and godly and grave, where nobody gets old and crafty and wise, where nobody gets old and bitter of tongue …

W.B. YEATS

I believe in everything until it's disproved. So I believe in fairies, the myths, dragons. It all exists, even if it's in your mind. Who's to say that dreams and nightmares aren't as real as the here and now? Reality leaves a lot to the imagination.

JOHN LENNON

A lady with whom I was riding in the forest
said to me that the woods always seemed
to her to wait, as if the genii who inhabit
them suspend their deeds until the
wayfarer had passed onward; a thought
which poetry has celebrated in the dance
of the fairies, which breaks off on the
approach of human feet.

RALPH WALDO EMERSON

And what if cheerful shouts
  at noon
Come, from the village sent,
Or song of maids, beneath
  the moon
With fairy laughter blent?

WILLIAM CULLEN BRYANT

If you see a fairy ring
In a field of grass,
Very lightly step around,
Tiptoe as you pass;
Last night fairies frolicked there,
And they're sleeping somewhere near.

WILLIAM SHAKESPEARE

Grey lichens, mid they hills of creeping thyme,
Grow like to fairy forests hung with rime;
And fairy money-pots are often found
That spring like little mushrooms out of ground,
Some shaped like cups and some in slender trim
Wine glasses like, that to the very rim
Are filled with little mystic shining seed.

JOHN CLARE

chapter 2
Anatomy of a Fairy

She is the fairies' midwife, and she comes
In shape no bigger than an agate-stone
On the fore-finger of an alderman,
Drawn with a team of little atomies
Athwart men's noses as they lie asleep ...

WILLIAM SHAKESPEARE, *ROMEO AND JULIET*

previous page: **A baby fairy, Berwick, from *Blackie's Childrens' Annual*, 1922, British**
A close examination of fairy anatomy should begin at a young age.
right: **Titania aloft, Arthur Rackham, from *Shakespeare's A Midsummer Night's Dream*, first published 1908, British**
Fairy queen Titania in all her miniature majesty.

The fairy folk

Fairies as we commonly imagine them are dainty, diminutive creatures; about the size of a butterfly, and equally delicate and dazzling. But the tales don't always reflect this view. Fairies of folklore are more sinister, with powers over the human race and forces of nature that belie their usual miniature stature. Many fairies combine a capricious nature with rapid shape-shifting potential that permits them to change size and figure on impulse. As the poet W. B. Yeats wrote, these beings, "who are not of heaven but of the earth … have no inherent form, but change according to their whim, or the mind that sees them." One canny little man reports to an Irish witness, "I am bigger than I appear to you now. We can make the old young, the big small, the small big."

Different orders of fairy folk have always taken varying shapes, sizes, and appearances, ranging from finger-tall flitting figurines to stout, toddler-sized old men. The noble *Sidhe*, the gentry of Ireland and the Scottish Highlands, and the *Tylwyth Teg* of Wales may appear as tall and shadowy astral projections—some say up to six feet (two meters) tall— with a matchless beauty appropriate to the awe they command. Scandinavian elves and temptresses from lake and forest are human-sized, all the better to interact with mortals. They might resemble the languid medieval maidens of the Pre-Raphaelite Brotherhood, painted reclining on rocks or around trees, garments slipping off, waiting to bind gullible knights with their spells.

right: The Fairy Troupe, postcard by Margaret W. Tarrant, c. 1934, British Fairies dressed in the blossoms of spring flowers.

Wee creatures

The massed ranks of Teutonic and Norse elves, called *Kleine Volk* in German, are always small. Brownies and household spirits who inhabit hearth and home also tend to be miniature, like the trooping, ring-dancing fairies of the Celtic countries, who may be three inches (75mm) tall according to witnesses. The tiniest beings in the Celtic tradition are Cornish *Muryans* (or ants), named to reflect their size. Commentators suggest that if cultures as diverse as the native inhabitants of Australia and North America envisage their spirit races as tiny, this may be a globally common means of contemplating departed souls—that is what fairies are often said to be.

Singleton spirits, such as Leprechauns are somewhat larger; they are reported to be about three-feet (one meter) tall, as are the Scandinavian and Teutonic dwarves and others such as the Cornish Knockers, who live underground in mines and caverns. Usually they are short, stout, ugly, and hairy or prematurely aged.

left: **The underground workers, H. J. Ford from *The Violet Fairy Book* edited by Andrew Lang, 1907, British**
Small and incredibly strong, dwarves are legendary miners.
next page: **The leprechaun or fairy shoemaker, Warwick Goble from *The Book of Fairy Poetry,* 1920, British**

Beautiful and beastly

Some fairies are more beautiful than mortals could possibly imagine, especially female spirits of the elements who lure young men. Others, such as trolls and thick-set goblins, are defined by their ugliness: a human being dies on spying the repulsive *Bugul Noz,* who dwells deep within the Breton woodland. But one should not judge a fairy by his cover: the twisted Hobgoblin is essentially benevolent to mankind, like the poor *Bugul Noz,* whose gentle, hospitable qualities are disguised by his hideousness. Seeing is not believing in fairyland: fay that seem beautiful by moonlight "young with unblemished skin and glorious dark hair," as a Cornish legend has it, may, when caught by daylight, be "old, wrinkled and liver-spotted."

I caught him at work one day, myself,
In the castle ditch where fox-glove grows, -
A wrinkled, wizen'd and bearded Elf,
Spectacles stuck on his pointed nose,
Silver buckles to his hose,
Leather apron - shoe in his lap -
"Rip-rap, tip-tap,
Tick-tack-too!
(A grasshopper on my cap!
Away the moth flew!)
Buskins for a fairy prince,
Brogues for his son -
Pay me well, pay me well,
When the job is done!"
The rogue was mine, beyond a doubt.
I stared at him, he stared at me;
"Servant Sir!" "Humph" says he,
And pull'd a snuff-box out.
He took a long pinch, look'd better pleased,
The queer little Lepracaun;
Offer'd the box with a whimsical grace, -
Pouf! He flung the dust in my face,
And while I sneezed,
Was gone!

WILLIAM ALLINGHAM, *THE LEPRECHAUN OR FAIRY SHOEMAKER*

Anatomical oddities

Since fairies do not belong to the familiar human or animal worlds, they are liberated from the workaday confining rules of flesh and blood. They might often flout givens of anatomy, such as symmetry: Scottish Peg Leg Jack, the *Fachan*, has only one of each limb or organ: a single eye, ear, arm, leg, arranged in a line down a pole-like body. Fairies often slip between combinations of characteristics: half-fish, half-bird, part-goat are surprisingly common blends. The mer people spectacularly embody this tendency —they are human from the waist up and fish beneath, so are able to inhabit two worlds. Whether they are saltwater or freshwater species, the composite of maid and fish—of breasts and hair, tail and scales—seems an especially alluring mixture for mortal men.

right: **The Mermaid queen, H. J. Ford from *The Orange Fairy Book* edited by Andrew Lang, 1906, British**
Mer-people are half-human. half-fish. and identifiable by their powerful tails.
next page: **The mischievous imp, Joyce Plumstead from *Holiday Stories, 1936,* British**

Fairy limbs

Fairy extremities may look stunted or notably long or distorted—especially elves' feet which make them perfect for kicking. The German *Kobold* may have feet where hands should be; and Latino matriarchal house spirits, the *Duende*, icicle-shaped fingers. The Italian *Folletto's* toes point backward, like those of the Brazilian wood spirit *Curupira*, to throw hunters off the trail, and the Norwegian *Fossegrim's* feet trail into a mist. The wee Breton and Cornish fairies have tiny webbed feet, appropriate in such sea-defined locations. In some shape-shifters, an odd limb—maybe a chicken foot or goat leg—is a clue to their real nature.

Changing body parts also indicate whether spirits are feeling mischievous or protective. Russia's home-dwelling *Domovoi* has thickly haired hands: when they feel soft and warm, good luck is on the way; when cold and bristly, watch out for misfortune. Scandinavian elfin maidens are bodiless from the back: they are "only to be looked at in front, and are therefore made hollow, like the inside of a mask," affirms Hans Christian Anderson. Sweden's lady of the forest, the *Skogsrå*, seems beautifully life-like, but, from the back, she's as hollow as the trunk of the tree she presides over; once she shows her back, she vanishes. In West Malaysia, the female of the *Langsuir* fairy tribe has a hollow at the nape of her neck, hidden by hair that tumbles to her feet.

Some Scandinavian Wood-wives have a give-away foreign part that upsets an otherwise convincing portrayal of perfect womanhood. A cow's or fox's tail peeking from beneath the skirt, perhaps. Mortals should never comment on the give-away sign. In one Swedish legend a young boy simply remarks politely that the lady's "petticoat" is showing, and she tucks away her tail, content to have kept face.

Hairy fairies

Certain spirits are defined by masses of lanky, straggly, or dripping hair. Dwarves are known for having long gray beards—even the females in some universes. Brownies are thought of as shaggy, wild-looking, and rather raggedy, like their Welsh cousin, the *Bwbach*. Some fairies have such a thick covering of hair that they might be taken for the animals they associate with. Think of the Scottish Highland brownie, the *Gruagach*, who guards cattle and sheep, or that South African *Tokolosh* sulking beside the stream, as black and hairy as a baby baboon. Also animal-like is Ireland's *Fear Durg,* whose stance and long hairy nose brings about the nickname "rat boy." Trolls are the most obvious example of a hairy fairy, with hirsute hands, feet, and head accompanying curiously unappealing faces. They are much more ugly than the Danish troll dolls with day-glo hair that became a worldwide collecting fad in the 1960s and 70s (much revived in recent years).

right: **Breton water fairies, E. Zieu, *Journal des Voyages,* 1896, French**
Eerie sylphs trail ghostly strands of long, dripping hair.
next page: **Trolls, Karl Heilig from *Der Jugend,* 1903, German**
Trolls are noted for their large heads and thick, shaggy hair.

Shedding the skin

Shetland Selkies and some mer folk are said to have a skin that can be put on or off according to their surroundings: for instance, you might catch them shedding their amphibian coverings to dance on the sand in the moonlight. If this "sea-dress" is mislaid or stolen, however, they must remain in mortal form, eking out a sad, meager life in a human home, longing to regain their true selves.

The mer-wife

"A story is told of an inhabitant of Unst, who, in walking on the sandy margin of a voe, saw a number of mermen and mermaids dancing by moonlight, and several seal-skins strewed beside them on the ground. At his approach they immediately fled to secure their garbs, and, taking upon themselves the form of seals, plunged immediately into the sea. But as the Shetlander perceived that one skin lay close to his feet, he snatched it up, bore it swiftly away, and placed it in concealment.

On returning to the shore he met the fairest damsel that was ever gazed upon by mortal eyes, lamenting the robbery, by which she had become an exile from her submarine friends, and a tenant of the upper world. Vainly she implored the restitution of her property; the man had drunk deeply of love, and was inexorable; but he offered her protection beneath his roof as his betrothed spouse. The merlady, perceiving that she must become an inhabitant of the earth, found that she could not do better than accept of the offer. This strange attachment subsisted for many years, and the couple had several children. The Shetlander's love for his merwife was unbounded, but his affection was coldly returned. The lady would often steal alone to the desert strand, and, on a signal being given, a large seal would make his appearance, with whom she would hold, in an unknown tongue, an anxious conference. Years had thus glided away, when it happened that one of the children, in the course of his play, found concealed beneath a stack of corn a seal's skin; and, delighted with the prize, he ran with it to his mother. Her eyes glistened with rapture—she gazed upon it as her own—as the means by which she could pass through the ocean that led to her native home.

She burst forth into an ecstasy of joy, which was only moderated when she beheld her children, whom she was now about to leave; and, after hastily embracing them, she fled with all speed towards the seaside. The husband immediately returned, learned the discovery that had taken place, ran to overtake his wife, but only arrived in time to see her transformation of shape completed—to see her, in the form of a seal, bound from the ledge of a rock into the sea. The large animal of the same kind with whom she had held a secret converse soon appeared, and evidently congratulated her, in the most tender manner, on her escape. But before she dived to unknown depths, she cast a parting glance at the wretched Shetlander, whose despairing looks excited in her breast a few transient feelings of commiseration.

"Farewell!" said she to him, "and may all good attend you. I loved you very well when I resided upon earth, but I always loved my first husband much better."

W.W. GIBBINGS, *FOLK-LORE AND LEGENDS, SCOTLAND*

Winged delight

Some to the Sun their Insect-Wings unfold,
Waft on the Breeze, or sink in Clouds of Gold,
Transparent Forms, too fine for mortal Sight,
Their fluid Bodies half dissolv'd in Light.
Loose to the Wind their airy Garments flew,
Thin glitt'ring Textures of the filmy Dew;
Dipt in the richest Tincture of the Skies,
Where Light disports in ever-mingling Dies,
While ev'ry Beam new transient Colors flings,
Colors that change whene'er they wave their Wings.

ALEXANDER POPE, *THE RAPE OF THE LOCK*

There are scant descriptions of little people with wings in folk tales. Gossamer wings became a defining fairy attribute only from the eighteenth century. It was the fairy artists and illustrators in the nineteenth century who crystallized the current vision of fairy—a theatrical confection of frothy tulle, gossamer, insect wings, and ballet slippers. They did this so thoroughly that 200 years on, this image still defines how the fay appear.

right: **A pretty pair of fairy wings, Warwick Goble from Charles Kingsley's *The Water Babies*, 1910, British**
The artist was inspired by the gosssamer iridescence of insect wings.

Flitting feathers

Japan's Shinto tree spirits, the *Ten-gu*, have feathered bird's wings (and beaks) adorning a humanoid form. Feathers are magic; often used in divination rituals—in Zanzibar they confer invisibility if plucked from the neck of a black chicken. From Japan comes the tale of a winged maiden who, like the Selkie, has shrugged off her "beautiful robe of pure white feathers" and hung it on a pine tree. A fisherman finds it and threatens not to return it:

The feather robe

"Oh," cried the maiden pitifully, "I cannot go soaring into the sky without my robe of feathers, for if you persist in keeping it I can never more return to my celestial home. Oh, good fisherman, I beg of you to restore my robe!" The fisherman, who must have been a hard-hearted fellow, refused to relent. "The more you plead," said he, "the more determined I am to keep what I have found." Thus the maiden made answer:

Speak not, dear fisherman! Speak not that word!
Ah! know'st thou not that, like the hapless bird
Whose wings are broke, I seek, but seek in vain,
Reft of my wings, to soar to heav'n's blue plain?

After further argument on the subject the fisherman's heart softened a little. "I will restore your robe of feathers," said he, "if you will at once dance before me." Then the maiden replied, "I will dance it here-the dance that makes the Palace of the Moon turn round, so that even poor transitory man may learn its mysteries. But I cannot dance without my feathers." "No," said the fisherman suspiciously. "If I give you this robe, you will fly away without dancing before me." This remark made the maiden extremely angry.

"The pledge of mortals may be broken," said she, "but there is no falsehood among the heavenly beings."

These words put the fisherman to shame, and, without more ado, he gave the maiden her robe of feathers.

When the maiden had put on her pure white garment she struck a musical instrument and began to dance, and while she danced and played she sang of many strange and beautiful things concerning her faraway home in the moon. She sang of the might Palace of the Moon, where thirty monarchs ruled, fifteen in robes of white when that shining orb was full, and fifteen robed in black when the moon was waning. As she sang and played and danced she blessed Japan, "that earth may still her proper increase yield!"

The fisherman did not long enjoy this kindly exhibition of the Moon Lady's skill, for very soon her dainty feet ceased to tap upon the sand. She rose into the air, the white feathers of her robe gleaming against the pine trees or against the blue sky itself. Up, up she went, still playing and singing, past the summits of the mountains, higher and higher, until her song was hushed, until she reached the glorious Palace of the Moon."

F. HADLAND DAVIS, *MYTHS AND LEGENDS OF JAPAN*

Auric wings

Fairy wings are described by some witnesses more as a wing-shaped aura of light than as physical essences. The notion of auras gained widespread currency across Europe and North America with the nineteenth-century Spiritualist movement. An aura is a subtle area surrounding the physical body seen by those suitably attuned as layers of radiance or color, a visual representation of an energy field linked to forces in the universe. The notion informed writers inspired by fairy lore, including Sir Arthur Conan Doyle, whose uncle, Richard Doyle, was one of the leading illustrators of fairy folk in household magazines and influential anthologies of fairy tales. Auric wings also recall descriptions of angel wings in the early mystic texts of the Jewish faith, especially in Enoch 2, where angels are described in terms that echo the popular conventions of fairy painting.

Sometimes the aura of a fairy is experienced not visually, but as a flame, a candle burning blue (a common notion in Shakespeare's time), or a distinct scent presence. As angels are sometimes noticed only by an inexplicable waft of incense, perfume being a sign of the divine, so too with some fairy visitations. In Cornwall an intense floral scent assails those who draw near a portal to fairyland, but it's not always as pleasant. Scottish sea fairies called *Nucklelavees* are accompanied by a smell of old fish and rotten eggs, betraying malicious intent.

left: **Unnamed artist in *Allers Familj Journal*, 1925, Swedish**
A fairy joins a colorful host of butterflies in an airy dance.

Butterfly fluttering

Why has the common image of a fairy consolidated around the image of butterfly wings? Butterflies, like fairies, are creatures of magical transformation. In its caterpillar skin, the creature grovels on the earth, like us mortals; then, after a time of death-like cocoon, she emerges into her full beauty, free to fly to a higher element. The flitting, darting, light-reflecting dragonfly, too, is transformed from a base watery element to the higher realm of air, so it is not surprising that dragonfly wings are also pictured adorning fairy forms.

Fairies are associated with dead souls in many traditions, and the soul has been envisaged in ancient Egypt and the classical world as a tiny being with wings that escapes to another place at death. The butterfly analogy seems appropriate. In ancient Greek and Latin and in Russian dialects the same words are used to describe the soul of the deceased and the butterfly. Maori and Aztec lore teaches that the soul returns to earth after death as a butterfly. Blackfoot Native Americans believe butterflies bring sleep and dreams, another fairy function across the globe. The "butter" element of the word in English, German, and Czech also relates to fairy lore, for these spirits are always associated with cows, milk, and cream. Fairy lore has congregated around moths, too—they are also regarded as departed souls. In Cornwall they are known as "Pisgies," a fairy name.

right: **Trying out new wings, Florence Mary Anderson, 1919, British**
The wish to be borne aloft on fairy wings is granted!

Beings of light

The most elevated or "fair," (a word once a synonym for beauty) of the fairy folk are often described as "shining" or opalescent in form. Ireland's legendary fairy race are known as the Luminous or Shining Ones for their magical knowledge and other-worldly grace. "White as the driven snow in moonlight" says a nineteenth-century witness of a fairy sighting. Other people testify to formless presences that show only as a whiteness, like some of the wailing Celtic death fairies. Spirits of the sea tend to reflect the play of light on its surface, the most astonishing being the Maori *Ponaturi*, whose skin has a phosphorescent glow at night.

Persian *Devas* and Italian *Candelas* are tiny spheres of light who appear as a group of tiny twinkles after dusk has descended. "Like dolls" said an Englishman describing his fairy sighting in 1842, "dresses sparkling as if with spangles but not solid, rather light and shadowy." Fairy light might be most apparent in the eyes, for many can tell a fairy by the eyes alone, which are strangely penetrating and bright, often described as more shining than ours, like burning fire coals in a pale visage. They recall the intently staring eyes of figures illustrated in the wonderful *Book of Kells,* the eyes of someone who sees beyond the present world.

Q. Can you describe one of the opalescent beings?
A. "The first of these I saw I remember very clearly, and the manner of its appearance: there was at first a dazzle of light, and then I saw that this came from the heart of a tall figure with a body apparently shaped out of half-transparent or opalescent air, and throughout the body ran a radiant, electrical fire, to which the heart seemed the center. Around the head of this being and through its waving luminous hair, which was blown all about the body like living strands of gold, there appeared flaming wing-like auras. From the being itself light seemed to stream outwards in every direction; and the effect left on me after the vision was one of extraordinary lightness, joyousness, or ecstasy."

W. Y. EVANS-WENTZ, TOLD BY AN IRISH MYSTIC, FROM *THE FAIRY-FAITH IN CELTIC COUNTRIES*

Fairy finery

Up the airy mountain,
Down the rushy glen,
We daren't go a-hunting
For fear of little men;
Wee folk, good folk,
Trooping all together,
Green jacket, red cap,
And white owl's feather!

WILLIAM ALLINGHAM, *THE FAIRIES*

Fairies come dressed in the colors of nature: the green of foliage and grass, the brown of soil and bark, the blue of sky and water, or the piercing whiteness of snow. Whatever color they wear, what is noted is the brightness or radiance of the costume. In Breton stories the gaudy hues fade the nearer you draw toward them. "Airy, flowing, and silken" are common words describing their robes in fairy collections from Wales to Denmark; in the French tradition, the flowing quality may obscure the sex of the tiny being inside. And some little folk are naked: Italy's trooping blind *Callicantzaroi* are tiny, slender, and completely bare.

right: Fairies and Pixies by Félix Lorioux, 1912, French
Lorioux used vivid, riotous colors for his fairy illustrations.

Scarlet Red clothing pretty much defines fairy folk, particularly in the form of a cap or waving feather. Irish fairies especially are referred to as "little red men." Red is a color of potent magic and of protection, since it confronts forces of darkness with a symbol of natural life force, blood, and the blazing sun. It is a liturgical color: in Italy the "little Monk" *Mona Ciello* wears a hooded long red cloak. It also is a sign of the heart, associated with seduction and love, and with the loose morals of the scarlet woman: spot the danger signs in the red and white clothing of the alluring water spirit *Mami Wata* on Africa's western coast, a mermaid who takes the form of an urban babe. The word "red" in a fairy name indicates danger: the fearsome Scottish borders Redcap dyes his headwear in human blood.

Green The second-most oft-cited color for fairy costume is green, states fairy historian Katherine Briggs, and is the usual dress of Scottish fairies according to a 1901 reporter. Green carries associations of fertility and the natural world. It is the color of the new life of spring and celebrations of May, the green month of the northern hemisphere. But it is also a color in Celtic lands associated with death (in nature green can be decay). Green is, naturally, the Leprechaun's color; one might nominate him patron saint of modern Ireland, alongside the same-hued shamrock.

left: **Fairy by Ida Rentoul Outhwaite, c. 1921, Australian**
Heathland fairies flit over moorland in gold-brown garments.

White Signifying purity and peace, moonlight and the magic of the moon goddess, this color is associated with the next life. Ghosts are white, and it is a sign of mourning across Asia. White is also a holiday color, far removed from the dark usefulness of everyday garments. White linen gowns were prized before the days of washing machines and bleach, and so are fit for a queen. The Irish *Sidhe* dress in a white that is almost blinding. Mother-of-pearl is an option for marine spirits. The Scottish lough-haunting sprite Shellycoat is named for his overcoat of shells that clatters as he ascends and descends the depths. When white is trimmed with blue, in the form of petticoats or headwear, it recalls the sky or celestial realm, just as the Blessed Virgin's link with blue underpins her higher spirituality.

Brown Fairies of the moorland wear "heath-brown" clothes in Scotland, dyed with lichen, while in one Shetland writer's experience, all fairies, male and female, wear workaday gray, with rough woolen mittens. Brown garments might be made from foliage or lichen by little brown men in Scotland and Cornwall. The Irish *Grogoch* sports a coating of twigs and dirt over his red hairy form. Teutonic Wood-wives weave coverings from moss and lichen for their gnarled, root-like limbs. The brown garments might be skin: the lambskin of the feared *Duergar* dwarves who lurk at the wayside, or the fur worn by *Salvani* wood nymphs.

Courtly costume Some accounts of fairies describe in loving detail their elaborate, exquisitely stitched costumes, fit on earth for nobles alone. The queen of the Irish *Sidhe* wears a gown of spun silver, as one might expect, but equally impressive is the clothing of tiny spirits going about mundane tasks, like the minuscule *Muryans*, or ant people, of Cornwall.

They put on lace and silver bells to visit the homes of the sick, doing good works, rather like Victorian gentry. In return for helping with household tasks or fetching the midwife, householders sometimes reward tiny cohabitees with new livery: a miniature suit of green that equips them to leave home and cavort with the trooping fairies.

Working attire Solitary fairies with a trade tend to wear scaled-down versions of the cobbler's or miner's outfit worn by mortal co-workers, complete with working paraphernalia: miniature hammers, picks and lamps for miners; anvils, hammers, and leather aprons for fairy smiths. Often the kit is strangely old-fashioned, the traditional garb of centuries before; almost a caricature or a collector's costume doll. In an Irish story related in Thomas Crofton Croker's *Fairy Legends and Traditions of 1825,* a woman spots, in a row of beans, a tiny brogue-maker, putting on the heel of a pump with a tick-tack, tick-tack of his hammer. She describes "a bit of an old man not a quarter so big as a new-born child, with a little cocked hat on his head, and a dudeen in his mouth smoking away, and a plain old-fashioned drab-colored coat with big buttons upon it on his back, and a pair of massy silver buckles in his shoes, that almost covered his feet, they were so big; and he working away as hard as ever he could, heeling a little pair of brogues."

Fairy vocal power

O, train me not, sweet mermaid, with thy note,
To drown me in thy sister's flood of tears:
Sing, siren, for thyself and I will dote:
Spread o'er the silver waves thy golden hairs,
And as a bed I'll take them and there lie,
And in that glorious supposition think
He gains by death that hath such means to die:
Let Love, being light, be drowned if she sink!

WILLIAM SHAKESPEARE, *THE COMEDY OF ERRORS*

Whether it is flaming breath, a keening wail, or entrancing song, that which emits from a fairy's mouth is alone enough to bewitch a mortal. A Welsh maiden describes being spellbound by tiny figures talking a language too beautiful to be repeated. The sounds might be rich and melodious or silvery secrets broadcast on the wind. The South African *Mbulu* draws his prey by creeping from a river, whispering gently to those who wend down the banks, for the very breath of a fairy is magical. If you pass too close to an invisible spirit, you might catch the "fairy wind," a disease of the skin caused by fairy breath.

left: **The Sirens, Gustave Moreau, 826–1898, French**
The haunting voices of sirens can be heard over the stormiest seas.

Doom songs

Weeping and a-wailing, the prophetess spirit who appears in voice form only to portend a death is common to many cultures. Her cry ranges from a low and fairly pleasant singing to the crashing of boards struck together or a piercing wail that shatters glass. She is best known as the Irish *Bean-sidhe,* or Banshee, who comes only once, the night before a death, keening and clapping.

In Scottish tradition she is the formless *Caointeach*, a wailing woman heard alongside glen and stream; in Wales *Cyhyraeth*, who rattles shuttered windows at a family home even when everyone has moved on. Spirit laughter, usually disembodied, always portends mischief, if not extreme danger. Be especially fearful when traveling alone at night in the mountainsides of Wales, for there lurks the *Gwyllian*, whose cackle belies her appearance as a kindly old woman.

The siren song of water spirits spills up from the depths to float on the waves, melting the heart of all who hear it. In Swedish inland waters the *Näcken* coax listeners with fiddle, flute, and horn. Add on the surpassing beauty of the Mermaid or female Merrow to create a dish no mortal can resist. Odysseus himself had to stop the ears of his crew with wax and lash his body to the ship's mast, as he knew how impossible is it for even the most noble of men to resist the lure of water spirits intent on capture.

right: The Banshee from *Elfin Song,* Florence Harrison, 1912, British
The wailing of this fearsome Irish fairy is theard the night before a death.

Naming the fair ones

There is a well-defined etiquette in discussing fairies. Never refer to the wee folk by name. To do so would be to court their wrath. Rather, use one of the many euphemisms—and make it a gracious one, such as "The Gentry," which cannot offend. One should never speak harshly of other folk, and that includes using harsh epithets. But just as talking of them with too much lightness can cause anger, so, too, does undue praise. It might be best simply to stay silent in places where the fay might be lurking, in woods and at crossroads, especially near nightfall.

Sometimes the name of a spirit derives from a word of disguise: the Norwegian woods-woman *Huldra* is named from a root meaning "secret" or "encovered." The power of a secret, or sacred, name empowers those who utter it with its attributes; this is established in all the world's great religions. If the name of a spirit is the spirit, then in stating it one brings it into being, and risks becomes it oneself. Polite epithets for fairies include the following:

By size:
small people: *in Cornwall*
wee folk: *in Ireland*
little people: *in Isle of Man*
little boys or fellas: *in Isle of Man*

By appearance:
little red men: *in Ireland*
green children: *English literary term*

By moral standing:
their mother's blessing: *in Wales*
godmothers: *in Brittany*
our good mothers: *in France*
good people: *in Ireland and Western Malaysia*
good folk: *in England, especially for Brownies*
good ladies: *in France*
good neighbors: *in France and Scotland*
honest folk: *in Ireland*
people of peace: *in Ireland*
women of peace: *Scotland*
children of pride: *in Isle of Man*
fair folk or family: *in Wales, Ireland and Scandinavia*

By nature:
still folk: *in Scotland*
silent-moving folk: *in Scotland*

By status:
gentry: *in Ireland*
blessed folk: *in Ireland*

By habitat:
fair family of the wood/mine: *in Wales*
hill folk: *in Ireland*

Of all the minor creatures of mythology, fairies are the most beautiful, the most numerous, the most memorable

ANDREW LANG

Mist-clad in the light of the moon
Starspun seekers – I search for thee!
Faery light – I ask thy boon
Of branch and thorn and Elder tree!
Wood woven creatures, shadow weavers
River keepers – come to me!
Just beyond reaching
Never in keeping
Spirits of Faery – I call unto thee!
Wind-hewn wildness
Dark and brightness
Spiral enchantments – born of the sky!
Cradle me with elven hands,
Abide with me, thy human child!

W.B. YEATS

If I were just a fairy small,
I'd take a leaf and sail away,
I'd sit astride the stem and guide
It straight to Fairyland – and stay.

BEN JONSON

chapter 3
A Fairy's Day

Hear the call!
Fays, be still!
Noon is deep
On vale and hill.
Stir no sound
The Forest round!
Let all things hush
That fly or creep, –
Tree and bush,
Air and ground,
Hear the call!
Silence keep!
One and all
Hush, and sleep!

WILLIAM ALLINGHAM, *THE NOON-CALL*

previous page: **Fairies on the shoreline, Warwick Goble from *The Water Babies,* 1910, British**
left: **Elves return home to sleep, Warwick Goble from *The Fairy Book,* 1923, British**
The wee folk gallivant all night and retire at first cock-crow.

Rising and retiring times

Then, my queen, in silence sad
Trip we after night's shade.
We the globe can compass soon,
Swifter than the wand'ring moon.

WILLIAM SHAKESPEARE, *A MIDSUMMER NIGHT'S DREAM*

Dusk and dawn are significant times for fairy folk, since their day is our night. These are liminal hours, when transition thins the boundaries between worlds—we may catch a glimpse of their universe, and they trespass into ours. The most powerful period for fairies is the witching hour, midnight, when they can be seen processing or riding. This is the traditional time to rescue mortals trapped in fairyland: grasp them as the clock strikes and hold tight till dawn, when the magic must end. Fairies retire at the crowing of the cock, symbol of the rising sun, in anticipation of the first rays of light. Sunlight can be quite a weapon, since fairies of all types are swallowed by it. Dwarves turn to stone. Those who fail to return home after cock crow are transformed to daystanders while the sun runs its course across the sky, only returning to fairyland once night falls.

right: **Titania asleep, Arthur Rackham, from *Shakespeare's A Midsummer Night's Dream,* first published 1908, British**
next page **Oberon and Titania, *A Midsummer Nights Dream,* Joseph Noel Paton, 1821–1900 British**

Fairy transport

Traditional tales tell of wee folk moving around in myriad ways, from bubbles to breezes to bats. But rarely with wings, unless they have hitched a ride on an insect, or a bird, as elves are likely to do. Some fairies get airborne by muttering incantations; should a mortal overhear the magic words and repeat them, he might be caught up in the chase. Shakespeare has Queen Mab riding in a carriage formed from two halves of a hazelnut (a magical fairy nut). In Michael Drayton's earlier poem *Nymphidia, the Court of Fairy*, the queen's coach is a snail shell and her attendants ride grasshoppers: many literary and arty fay are insect-driven.

Her wagon spokes made of long spinner's legs,
The cover, of the wings of grasshoppers;
Her traces, of the smallest spider web;
Her collars, of the moonshine's wat'ry beams;
Her whip, of cricket's bone; the lash, of film;
Her wagoner, a small grey-coated gnat ...

WILLIAM SHAKESPEARE, *ROMEO AND JULIET*

right: **Hitching a ride on a butterfly, Warwick Goble from *The Fairy Book,* 1923, British**
Fairies show endless ingenuity in their transport modes.
next page: **Fairies Floating Downstream in a Peapod, Amelia Jane Murray, 1800–96, British**

I do come about the coppes
Leaping upon flowers toppes;
Then I get upon a Flie,
Shee carries me abouve the skie,
And trip and goe.

MICHAEL DRAYTON, *NYMPHIDIA*

above: **Elves riding on dragonflies, Cora E.M. Paterson, from *Holiday Stories*, 1936, British**
left: **A jaunt on a butterfly by Félix Lorioux, 1912, French**

Riding the air waves

Fairies swim in the air according to the Scottish fairy writer Robert Kirk, though he does not detail the mechanism. Some spirits hitch a ride on the wind, like Italy's flitting *Folletti*, who are tiny and light enough to ride the gusts. In the river Elbe, water sprites known as *Otteermaaner* or *Alven* enwrap themselves in bubbles of air in the water and by this means move around. Other fairies borrow the broomstick method from witch lore, flying on a shaft or bundle of grass or straw, even a cabbage stalk. Orkney fairies ride bulwands, stems of the dock plant—at great speed.

And they are elfin mariners
Who stand at prow and helm
By mortal eye unseen, they hie
From many an airy realm

FLORENCE HARRISON, *ELFIN SONG*

right: **A ship of the sky, from *Elfin Song,* Florence Harrison, 1912, British**
A fairy sails at the helm of a cloud-borne ship.

Fairy horsemen

Many fairy people get about on horseback, but it is the Irish fairies who
are defined by a passion for riding. They are famed for fairy steeds that
gallop faster than the wind and can carry riders over land, lake, or sea.
The processing of the mounted gentry army is another impressive sight,
moving in its thousands by moonlight, armor shining. If the cavalcade is
not seen, it might be sensed in an unearthly aura of wildness and the
chinking of massed bridles. Even when unseen and unheard, there might
be evidence of processing fairies, for they are said to steal mortal steeds.
If a groom comes to the stables in the early morning to find a horse
panting, fatigued, and covered in foam, he can guess where it has been.

**The fairies take great delight in horsemanship, and are
splendid riders. Many fine young men are enticed to ride
with them, when they dash alone with the fairies like the
wind, Finvarra himself leading, on his great black horse
with the red nostrils, that look like flames of fire.
And ever after the young men are the most fearless riders
in the country, so the people know at once that they have
hunted with the fairies.**

**And the breed of horses they reared could not be
surpassed in the world—fleet as the wind, with the
arched neck and the broad chest and the quivering**

nostril, and the large eye that showed they were made of fire and flame, and not of dull, heavy earth. And the Tuatha made stables for them in the great caves of the hills, and they were shod with silver and golden bridles, and never a slave was allowed to ride them. A splendid sight was the cavalcade of the *Tuatha-de-Danann* knights. Seven-score steeds, each with a jewel on his forehead like a star, and seven-score horsemen, all the sons of kings, in their green mantles fringed with gold, and golden helmets on their head, and golden greaves on their limbs, and each knight having in his hand a golden spear.

LADY WILDE, *ANCIENT LEGENDS OF IRELAND*

Enchanted horses

The Celts know all about fairies and their horses. In Wales there are many terrifying legends of semi-spectral Water Horses (*Ceffyl-dwr*)—usually, these are creatures that emerge from rivers and offer to carry weary travelers. After flying for great distances in the air, these fairy steeds vanish into thin air at a dizzying height above the ground, leaving the hapless rider to plummet to his or her death.

They have similar creatures in Scotland. There, it was common for the Water Horse to wait invitingly for a rider on the shore of a river or loch. Once mounted, the horse would dive into the water and drown the person on its back. In Scotland these fairy horses are often known as Kelpies; all children would be warned not to accept rides from these strange, magic horses—otherwise the unhappy children would find themselves riding to a home beneath the waves, whence they would be unlikely to return.

right: Lantern slide from the series *Gossip about Fairies,* 19th century
The terrified children are mounted on a fairy horse that has run away with them, and is plunging beneath the waves, where they will all drown.

Fairy feasting

Instead of a crust a peacock pie,
Instead of bone sweet venison,
Instead of a groat a white lily
With seven blooms thereon.

And each fair cup was deep with wine:
Such was the changeling's charity
The sweet feast was enough for nine,
But not too much for three.

O toothsome meat in jelly froze!
O tender haunch of elfin stag!
Oh, rich the odour that arose!
Oh, plump with scraps each bag!

WALTER DE LA MARE, *THE THREE BEGGARS*

left: **A peacock pie, Warwick Goble from *The Book of Fairy Poetry*,
1920, British**
The fairy has transformed a hard crust of bread into a magical feast.
next page: **An elfin cook, Cora E.M. Paterson, from *Holiday Stories*,
1936, British**

Fairy food

In his famous treatise on fairy lore, Robert Kirk explains that fairy food varies according to the nature of the spirit. "Some fairies have bodies so spongeous thin and dessicate that they can feed only by sucking on fine spirituous liquor that appears like pure air or oil." One might count the Persian *Perie* among them, who survive, like supermodels, by sipping scent, as befits their gossamer-light form. Others—such as Brownies—are altogether more earthy and dine on grosser substances. Kirk says they prey on grain as do crows and mice, sometimes grinding it to bake bread. Some reports describe how when borrowing human fare, from a sip of milk to an entire sheep, the fay consume only the essence—the life-force, or nutritious part of the foodstuff—leaving for mortal consumption its outward semblance or appearance. Irish lore dictates that neither man nor beast (not even pigs) should finish up food left overnight for the fairies, because it no longer has substance.

Certain foodstuffs fairies consider their own by right: milk spilt from the churn coming to or from the dairy, butter that sticks on the knife after cutting, and fallen cattle. English, Welsh, and Scots fairies, and even Scandinavian elves, are inordinately fond of butter. Welsh fay adore cheese also: lumps should be cast into a spring or lake to propitiate them, and a really big, round, handsome cheese might even woo them into mortal wedlock.

Spirits of the home appreciate a bowl of fresh milk nightly, and some good white bread (no old crusts, or leftovers). Saffron-infused milk would be even better, for saffron is highly prized by little folk. They might also like a wee dram of something and a bit of baccy, and object to teetotal preachers and other abstainers (sometimes with malice).

Never share a fairy feast; and when in fairyland taste no morsel of the sumptuous offerings nor drop of ruby red wine, or you will remain bewitched for ever. This taboo extends beyond the Celtic world, into Polynesian and Maori fairy lore. If you are what you eat, to partake of the fairy will make you of the fairy, too. Those who *do* eat find themselves strangely unsated, no matter how much they gorge. Or, as in a Canadian tale, having tasted one mouthful from a fairy plate, they are unable to stop eating, and fear they must burst.

Enchanting music

The treble was a three-mouthed grasshopper,
Well-tutored by a skilful chorister:
An ancient master, that did use to play
The friskings which the lambs do dance in May.
And long time was the chiefest called to sing,
When on the plains the fairies made a ring;
Then a field-cricket, with a note full clean,
Sweet and unforced and softly sung the mean,
To whose accord, and with no mickle labor,
A pretty fairy played upon a tabor:
The case was of a hazel-nut, the heads
A bat's wing dressed, the snares were silver threads;
A little stiffened lamprey's skin did suit
All the rest well, and served them for a flute;
And to all these a deep well-breasted gnat,
That had good sides, knew well his sharp and flat,
Sung a good compass, making no wry face, ⁻
Was there as fittest for a chamber-bass.
These choice musicians to their merry king
Gave all the pleasures which their art could bring.

WILLIAM BROWNE, *THE FAIRY MUSICIANS*

Music plays such an important part in a fairy's day, particularly that of a Celtic fairy, that some wee folk like the Hebridian spinning fairy, the *Loireag*, punish humans who can't hold a tune. Haunting, lilting, and utterly other-worldly, fairy music, once caught by human ears, is so bewitching, one loses one's senses. Whether it comprises sweetly melancholic airs that fix the hearer to the spot, or lively tunes that cause the body to start dancing, this music can remain in the mind forever, though it is impossible to recall the melody or quite remember the words. English composer Thomas Wood described listening to fairy music for some 20 minutes in 1922, and was struck by its harmonic structure. Rather than featuring a melody that led from and to somewhere, it was more vertical, he said, a stacking of tenuous sounds, woven together overhead, faint as a breath.

Fairy instruments are exquisitely tuned to the cultural tastes of the mortals who listen to them: in Wales, the little people play golden harps, in Ireland miniature fiddles, in Scotland the pipes. They can make music on more uncommon instruments, too: fishing nets and silver branches, even a hammer on an anvil. What is constant is the ability, when fairy fingers run over an instrument, to create sounds that will cause a listener's hair to stand on end. St Patrick himself was reputedly so entranced by the tunes of fairy musician Cascorach that he declared, "but for a twang of the fairy spell that infests it … nothing could more nearly than it resemble Heaven's harmony."

Musical encounters

Some humans claim to have learnt their art from supernatural tutors, perhaps by practicing at sessions in fairy dance halls, or as a thank you for a good deed done. The Swedish water *Näcken* is a master fiddler famed for passing on his skills (though he has been known to drown pupils, requiring remuneration). Or like Turlough O'Carolan, Ireland's finest harp composer, one could brave a night on a fairy *rath*. If sleeping here doesn't drive you senseless, it produces bardic skills. On the Isle of Eigg in the Scottish Hebrides still stands a fairy hill where one can lend an ear and learn new tunes. Similarly in the Isle of Man: lie with one ear close to Dalby Mountain to hear murmurs of infinity.

Some fairy folk rely on human players to fuel their dance sessions. If they don't come willingly, like Orcadian fiddler Davie o'Teeveth, who would gladly play for the peerie folk, then the fay must entice musicians below for a year and a day (the fiddler believes he has played one short session). He might return to the mortal world with an embarrassment of riches if he pleased the fairies, or with a supply of new tunes. The famous Scottish piper family, the MacCrimmons, were said to have gained their family musical inheritance from fairy tuition, and three haunting tunes of fairy provenance from separate sources can be found in the *Shetland Folk Book* (volume 2).

preceding pages 127–129: **Illustrations from *Elfin Song,* Florence Harrison, 1912, British**
right: **Botttom and Titania, illustration for *Shakespeare's A Midsummer Night's Dream,* Paul Thuman, 1834–1908, German**

Auspicious fairy days

The Celts divided the year into four parts, with each new year beginning on November 1, the first day of winter. Summer started on May 1. Between these sat important quarter days: midsummer and midwinter. These times of change, when the universe was thought to revolve and tight-locked borders would open, were considered thin or liminal. Access to other worlds was possible and fairies more likely to cross into our realm. The last night of each quarter of the year—the eves before powerful days broke at midnight—were thought especially magic, or rife. They still are, for this is when we hold our most popular celebrations invoking the fairy realm: Hallowe'en and Christmas Eve.

Robert Kirk reports that little folk move to new lodgings at the beginning of each quarter of the year. Those with second sight might have terrifying encounters with them, even in public, for they brazenly steal the vulnerable on these days. Other people report that on the last day of each quarter, fairy palaces are decked to their finest and especially welcoming to humans who fancy joining the celebrations. The days on which one should take care multiplied in 1752 when the Julian calendar was abandoned in western Europe for the Gregorian calendar, with the loss of 11 days. May Day moved to 12 May in effect. To be extra sure of covering all possible times when the doors to fairyland might be wide open, both days were celebrated, with festivities to protect the most open times: dawn, twilight, and midnight.

left: **Fairies celebrating, from *Elfin Song,* Florence Harrison, 1912, British**

Dates for your fairy calendar

1 February: Candlemas Eve; Celtic festival of Imbolc

Marks the half point to spring and the return of light in the northern hemisphere.

- Be sure to monitor all that travels over the threshold, in and out.
- Light protective candles and fires.

21 March: Old New Year's Day

24 April: St Mark's Eve

The night to watch for spirits in a churchyard and try love divination. Those born on this day can see fairies, it is said.

30 April: May Eve

Fairies favor this night for fighting. Carry out all protective measures before sunrise.

- Wear a crown of elder twigs to see fairies.
- Don't sit beneath a hawthorn at dusk or you will be enchanted.
- Place a lump of cold coal beneath a cradle.
- Protect milk churns, for milk theft on this night sets a precedent for the year.

11 May: Old May Eve

23 June: Midsummer Eve

The most celebratory time of year for fairies and a good night for divination.

- Stay clear of the hawthorn at dusk for fear of enchantment.
- Pick St John's wort on Midsummer Day and pin above the door for protection.

29 July: Eve of Celtic festival of Lughnasadh

Time to offer harvest fruit to propitiate the spirits.

31 October: Hallowe'en; Eve of Celtic festival of Samhain

A night for fortune telling and divination; don't forget to leave out food and drink for the spirits.

- Avoid the hawthorn at dusk, when fairy enchantment is strong.
- Avoid sloes and blackberries after this date, when the fairies pee on the bushes while flying, causing fruit to rot.

11 November: Old All Hallow's Eve
24 December: Christmas Eve

At Yule Eve, Norse ancestor spirits must be welcomed into the home, so unlock doors and windows.

- Bring in mistletoe, special for the fairies.

31 December: New Year's Eve

Traditional time for supernatural divination, license, and gift-giving.

Other special times

Friday: in Ireland considered the day on which fairy power is at its strongest or most mischievous, so a bad day to start a new venture, get married, or travel far.

Full moon: time of bright moonlight, which some fairies favor, such as the Portuguese Moors.

Stormy days: wild stormy nights when streams turn into torrents and the wind moans over moors are times when fairies might be flying; a shower could bring them to earth.

Church festivals: in Russia, people might expect to see spirits on Easter Sunday and the Thursday preceding it, and Ascension Day.

17 March: St Patrick's Day and the first day of spring in northern Scotland. The day to spot Leprechauns, ubiquitous in Irish bars the world over. Be sure to wear a shamrock.

The spirit of Christmas

On the night before Christmas the only creatures stirring in the modern house are benevolent fairies distributing toys to children. Over the years European regional traditions of flying witches and beneficent saints have mixed, matched, and changed days to bring us the ubiquitous figure who dominates schools and stores, TV and press for a good six weeks of the year: Father Christmas or Santa Claus. In the jolly old elf of Clement Clarke Moore's 1822 poem, *An Account of a Visit from St. Nicholas,* centuries of fairy lore is gathered: white beard, red costume, flying through the night sky and pounding on rooftops, tinkling bells, deer (fond of that iconic hallucinogenic fairy fungi, the red and white Fly Agaric mushroom).

Santa has gained a workforce of industrious worker fairies: little green-clad elves, diligent as dwarves who help make and wrap his gifts, and fill the sleigh, recall legends of the Nordic farm-dwelling *Nisse.* St. Nick also has links with the hearth spirit with his trips down the chimney, propitiated by cookies and mince pies, a tot of something warming, and a bowl of water and carrot, or regional porridge, for the helpers. He is proof that even the most cynical of us welcome fairies into the heart of the home at certain times of year.

right: **Christmas Fairies, unknown artist, 19th century, English**
Fairies waft around the head of a sleeping child on Christmas Eve.
next page: **Gnomes decking the tree, unknown artist,c. 1900**
Two jolly gnomes make themselves useful in traditional fashion.

The magic of Hallowe'en

**Heigh ho for hallowe'en
When the fairies a' are seen,
Some black and some green
Heigh ho for hallowe'en**

TRADITIONAL RHYME

This is the Eve on which Celtic peoples believed that the souls of those who had died in the year were able to pass to the other world, and every part of that other world was abroad to aid in the traveling and passing on. We mortals helped them along with feasting, bonfires to light the way, and food and drink left outdoors as offerings to members of the wandering fairy world (now represented in the form of marauding bands of trick or treaters).

The inveterate Irish fairy tale collector Lady Wlde recounts a wonderful tale about November Eve:

November Eve

There was a man of the village who stayed out late one November Eve fishing, and never thought of the fairies until he saw a great number of dancing lights, and a crowd of people hurrying past with baskets and bags, and all laughing and singing and making merry as they went alone.

"You are a merry set, he said, where are ye all going to?"

"We are going to the fair," said a little old man with a cocked hat and a gold band round it. "Come with us, Hugh King, and you will have the finest food and the finest drink you ever set eyes upon."

"And just carry this basket for me, said a little red-haired Woman."

So Hugh took it, and went with them till they came to the fair, which was filled with a crowd of people he had never seen on the island in all his days. And they danced and laughed and drank red wine from little cups. And there were pipers, and harpers, and little cobblers mending shoes, and all the most beautiful things in the world to eat and drink, just as if they were in a king's palace. But the basket was very heavy, and Hugh longed to drop it, that he might go and dance with a little beauty with long yellow hair, that was laughing up close to his face.

"Well, here put down the basket," said the red-haired woman, "for you are quite tired, I see;" and she took it and opened the cover, and out came a little old man, the ugliest, most misshapen little imp that could be imagined.

"Ah, thank you, Hugh," said the imp, quite politely; "you have carried me nicely; for I am weak on the limbs—indeed I have nothing to speak of in the way of legs: but I'll pay you well, my fine fellow; hold out your two hands."

And the little imp poured down gold and gold and gold into them, bright golden guineas. "Now go," said he, "and drink my health, and make yourself quite pleasant, and don't be afraid of anything you see and hear."

So they all left him, except the man with the cocked hat and the red sash round his waist.

"Wait here now a bit," says he, "for Finvarra, the king, is coming, and his wife, to see the fair."

As he spoke, the sound of a horn was heard, and up drove a coach and four white horses, and out of it stepped a grand, grave gentleman all in black and a beautiful lady with a silver veil over her face.

"Here is Finvarra himself and the queen," said the little old man; but Hugh was ready to die of fright when Finvarra asked:

"What brought this man here?"

And the king frowned and looked so black that Hugh nearly fell to the ground with fear. Then they all laughed, and laughed so loud that everything seemed shaking and tumbling down from time laughter. And the dancers came up, and they all danced round Hugh, and tried to take his hands to make him dance with them.

"Do you know who these people are; and the men and women who are dancing round you?" asked the old man. "Look well, have you ever seen them before?"

And when Hugh looked he saw a girl that had died the year before, then another and another of his friends that he knew had died long ago; and then he saw that all the dancers, men, women, and girls, were the dead in their long, white shrouds. And he tried to escape from them, but could not, for they coiled round him, and danced and laughed and seized his arms, and tried to draw him into the dance, and their laugh seemed to pierce through his brain and kill him. And he fell down before them there, like one faint from sleep, and knew no more till he found himself next morning lying within the old stone circle by the fairy rath on the hill. Still it was all true that he had been with the fairies; no one could deny it, for his arms were all black with the touch of the hands of the dead, the time they had tried to draw him into the dance; but not one bit of all the red gold, which the little imp had given him, could he find in his pocket. Not one single golden piece; it was all gone for evermore.

And Hugh went sadly to his home, for now he knew that the spirits had mocked him and punished him, because he troubled their revels on November Eve—that one night of all the year when the dead can leave their graves and dance in the moonlight on the hill, and mortals should stay at home and never dare to look on them.

LADY WILDE, *ANCIENT LEGENDS, MYSTIC CHARMS, AND SUPERSTITIONS OF IRELAND*

By the moon we sport and play,
With the night begins our day:
As we frisk the dew doth fall;
Trip it lightly, urchins all!
Lightly as the little bee,
Two by two and three by three,
And about we go, and about go we!

WILLIAM SHAKESPEARE

When I sound the fairy call,
Gather here in silent meeting,
Chin to knee on the orchard wall,
Cooled with dew and cherries eating.
Merry, merry,
Take a cherry;
Mine are sounder,
Mine are rounder,
Mine are sweeter.
For the eater
When the dews fall.
And you'll be fairies all.

ROBERT GRAVES

The fairies break their dances
And leave the printed lawn,
And up from India glances
The silver sail of dawn.

The candles burn their sockets,
The blinds let through the day,
The young man feels his pockets
And wonders what's to pay.

A.E. HOUSMAN

chapter 4
Helpful Spirits

Early to bed

But people should not sit up too late; for time fairies like to gather round the smoldering embers after the family are in bed, and drain the wine-cup, and drink the milk which a good house-wife always leaves for them, in case the fairies should come in and want their supper. A vessel of pure water should also be left for them to bathe in, if they like. And in all things the fairies are fond of being made much of, and flattered and attended to; and the fairy blessing will come back in return to the giver for what-ever act of kindness he has done to the spirits of the hill and the cave. Some unexpected good fortune or stroke of luck will come upon his house or his children; for the fairy race is not ungrateful, and is powerful over man both for good amid evil.

LADY WILDE, *ANCIENT LEGENDS, MYSTIC CHARMS, AND SUPERSTITIONS OF IRELAND*

previous page: **Fairy food, P. Kauffmann from *La Vieille Poupee*, c. 1890, French**
Fairies feed an earth-child on night-mist flavored with the scent of flowers.
right: ***Bwca'r Trwyn*, Doris Williamson & Constance E Rowlands, from *Wonder Tales of Ancient Wales*, 1921, British**
The Welsh house-goblin eagerly waits for his dish of cream.

Friendly dwarves

Snow White (or Snowdrop as she was originally known) fled from her wicked stepmother, and found sanctuary in a delightful little house with a troupe of dwarves. After working all day in the mines, they returned home to find her fast asleep. Overcome with pity, they let her sleep.

In the morning Snowdrop awoke, but when she saw the seven little Dwarfs she felt very frightened. But they were so friendly and asked her what her name was in such a kind way, that she replied: 'I am Snowdrop.'

ANDREW LANG, *THE RED FAIRY BOOK*

right: Snowdrop wakes up, Warwick Goble from *The Fairy Book*, 1923, British

Tiny and talented

Dwarves are highly gifted. They transform base metal and stone into precious objects—fine jewels, quality weapons and armor. They make some of the most powerfully magic items of the Norse gods, the legendary spear, golden ring, and hammer. This explains why they inspire such awe. Dwarves can choose to pass on some of their unrivalled skills to mortals. If a Celtic smith were to find creatures at work on his anvil, he could compel them to bless him with the secrets of the craft, or to attend him, when called, to complete tasks. Alternatively, dwarves might curse the items they make, much like the other underground metalworkers of Norse legend, the Dark *Alfs,* who bring about only misfortune.

In German tales dwarves are generous and especially helpful to neighbors in need. Mortals come to dwarf mountains to borrow kitchen implements, tableware, and festive dress for weddings, which the dwarves provide before the sun's rays hit the human world, in return for a portion of the feast. Yet, despite this generosity, in many tales dwarves are mocked by mankind and forced to abandon their glorious underground palaces.

The Cornish Knockers guide miners who share their "croust" to valuable seams of tin or other precious metals by knocking on the wall, or setting up a violent pounding when mines are about to cave in. The Welsh equivalent is the *Coblynau.* Since so many Cornish miners left home to work the mines of the New World, it is not surprising that another cousin, Tommy-Knocker, can be heard distinctly in American mines. But the Atlantic crossing may have turned his head, since he is best known for vengeful, malicious behavior, snuffing out candles, stealing tools, and leading miners astray.

Many hundreds of years ago … they often came out from their grotesque rocky palaces, seeking out people in house and field, in kitchen and spinning room, willing and ready to lend a helping hand in all sorts of household activities. Sometimes they helped the very poor with gold and precious stones, raising them up from their poverty; sometimes they provided helpful advice and told entertaining tales to the boys and girls, relating poetic mysteries, such as those of Paris. Further, the harmless creatures asked of the farmers and mountain inhabitants no other payment for their services than permission to come into the little corner of an inhabitant's living room: Here, next to the warm stove, they could spend the night on a little bundle of straw or on their own mountain jar of Asbetis when the winter cold would push into the deepest palace halls of the underworld and turn the springs and brooks to ice.

AUGUST SCHNEZLER, *THE DWARVES' CAVERN NEAR HASEL*

Elves spinning and stitching

In Scandinavian and Teutonic lore elves make fine spinners; whether this stems from sheer industriousness or magical prowess is left to conjecture. In Italy the *Gianes* elves enchant as they work, spinning pictures in the wheel to tell fortunes as they tease out the thread. The Grimm brothers' *Rumpelstiltzkin*, like the elf in many similar tales, can turn a hall piled high with straw into skeins of gold overnight.

There are many tales of industrious whirring coming from the spinning wheel or loom when householders are in bed. Superstition advises spinners to remove the band from the wheel before retiring (with a prayer), should a stray spirit, such as Russia's old lady spinner, the *Marui*, undo good work or cast spells into a weave. Women in Central Asia might feel the urge to unpick work next morning in regions where *Djinn* are known to fiddle with the loom.

Habetrot is a northern British fairy deformed by her industrious spinning; she helps maidens finish work if they keep her identity secret, for weaving and spinning, like fiddling and smithing, are traditionally seen as supernatural gifts. In some tales human craftsmen leave work unfinished at night to find it completed and neatly pressed next morning, as told in the well-known Grimm story, *The Elves and the Shoemaker.*

Leprechauns are fine cobblers, said to work purely on elfin shoes (they are only ever seen with one shoe of a pair). They work with tiny hammers, nails, and lasts on softest leather, borrowing materials from men, and leaving in recompense tokens of fortune. Sometimes they are spotted drunk, but never so far gone that they cannot complete a day's work.

Suddenly the door opened, and in stepped a tiny little man and said: "Good-evening, Miss Miller-maid; why are you crying so bitterly?" "Oh!" answered the girl, "I have to spin straw into gold, and haven't a notion how it's done." "What will you give me if I spin it for you?" asked the manikin. "My necklace," replied the girl. The little man took the necklace, sat himself down at the wheel, and whir, whir, whir, the wheel went round three times, and the bobbin was full. Then he put on another, and whir, whir, whir, the wheel went round three times, and the second too was full; and so it went on till the morning, when all the straw was spun away, and all the bobbins were full of gold.

ANDREW LANG, *RUMPELSTILTZKIN*

next page: **Rumpelstiltzkin, Margaret Evans Price, from *Once Upon a Time*, 1921, American**
Rumpelstiltztkin makes short work of spinning straw into gold.

Their women are said to spin, very finely, to dye, to tissue and embroider; but whether it be as [a] manual operation of substantial refined stuffs with apt and solid instruments, or only curious cobwebs, impalpable rainbows and a fantastic imitation of the actions of more terrestrial mortals, since it transcended all the senses of the seer to discern whither, I leave to conjecture

ROBERT KIRK, *THE SECRET COMMONWEALTH OF ELVES, FAUNS AND FAIRIES*

right: **Elves and shoemaker, George Cruikshank, *Popular German Stories,* c. 1865, British**

These kindly elves rescued a poor shoemaker, who rewarded them with beautiful new clothes—much to their delight.

The elves and the shoemaker

A shoemaker, by no fault of his own, had become so poor that at last he had nothing left but leather for one pair of shoes. So in the evening, he cut out the shoes which he wished to begin to make the next morning, and as he had a good conscience, he lay down quietly in his bed, commended himself to God, and fell asleep. In the morning, after he had said his prayers, and was just going to sit down to work, the two shoes stood quite finished on his table. He was astounded, and knew not what to say to it. He took the shoes in his hands to observe them closer, and they were so neatly made that there was not one bad stitch in them, just as if they were intended as a masterpiece. Soon after, a buyer came in, and as the shoes pleased him so well, he paid more for them than was customary, and, with the money, the shoemaker was able to purchase leather for two pairs of shoes. He cut them out at night, and next morning was about to set to work with fresh courage; but he had no need to do so, for, when he got up, they were already made, and buyers also were not wanting, who gave him money enough to buy leather for four pairs of shoes. The following morning, too, he found the four pairs made; and so it went on constantly, what he cut out in the evening was finished by the morning, so that he soon had his honest independence again, and at last became a wealthy man. Now it befell that one evening not long before Christmas, when the man had been cutting out, he said to his wife, before going to bed, "What think you if we were to stay up to-night to see who it is that lends us this helping hand?" The woman liked the idea, and lighted a candle, and then they hid themselves in a corner of the room, behind some clothes which were hanging up there, and watched. When it was midnight, two pretty little naked men came, sat down by the shoemaker's table, took all the work which was cut out before them and began to stitch, and sew, and hammer so skillfully and so quickly with their little fingers that the shoemaker could not turn away his eyes for astonishment. They did not stop until all was done, and stood finished on the table, and they ran quickly away.

Next morning the woman said, "The little men have made us rich, and we really must show that we are grateful for it. They run about so, and have nothing on, and must be cold. I'll tell thee what I'll do: I will make them little shirts, and coats, and vests, and trousers, and knit both of them a pair of stockings, and do thou, too, make them two little pairs of shoes." The man said, "I shall be very glad to do it;" and one night, when everything was ready, they laid their presents all together on the table instead of the cut-out work, and then concealed themselves to see how the little men would behave. At midnight they came bounding in, and wanted to get to work at once, but as they did not find any leather cut out, but only the pretty little articles of clothing, they were at first astonished, and then they showed intense delight. They dressed themselves with the greatest rapidity, putting the pretty clothes on, and singing,

"Now we are boys so fine to see,
Why should we longer cobblers be?"

Then they danced and skipped and leapt over chairs and benches. At last they danced out of doors. From that time forth they came no more, but as long as the shoemaker lived all went well with him, and all his undertakings prospered.

JACOB AND WILHELM GRIMM, *HOUSEHOLD TALES*

Guardians of the home

Helpful domestic spirits make their homes under hearth and on hob, borrowing and lending silverware and other useful items, and doing favors in return for warmth, shelter, and the comfort of good food, drink, and company. Peep through a crack in the kitchen door one night, while everyone sleeps, and you might spy, as did Welsh maid Catti Jones, "a jolly company of *ellyllon*, working away like mad, and laughing and dancing as madly as they worked." These benign household spirits still inhabit our kitchens, if only in the guise of dish detergents such as Fairy Liquid, and pastry shortenings such as Cookeen!

The maid having swept the kitchen, makes a good fire the last thing at night, and having put the churn, filled with cream, on the whitened hearth, with a basin of fresh cream for the *Bwbach* on the hob, goes to bed to await the event. In the morning she finds (if she is in luck) that the *Bwbach* has emptied the basin of cream, and plied the churn-dasher so well that the maid has but to give a thump or two to bring the butter in a great lump.

WIRT SIKES, *BRITISH GOBLINS: WELSH FOLK-LORE, FAIRY MYTHOLOGY, LEGENDS AND TRADITIONS*

left: **Elfin gifts, Gustaf Tenggren, Good *Housekeeping,* 1927, Swedish** Silverware is traditionally loaned and borrowed by elves and humans.

Hidden housekeepers

House spirits watch over a family and help with household tasks, finishing up what remains undone at the end of a busy day, especially at times of stress and illness, such as harvest-time. They keep house and occupants safe from fire and robbery by groaning or knocking, perhaps, or by provoking a dog to bark or horses to stamp, waking a sleeping master or mistress. But only, this must be stressed, when shown proper respect. One should tidy up before they "do," as one would for a fastidious cleaner (especially for the Welsh *Bwbach*), and keep them warm and well-fed with choice offerings.

Ireland's fairy housekeeper, the *Bean Tighe,* materializes in the form of a kindly old lady with plump cheeks, who completes chores at night and is especially fond of caring for harassed mothers of young children (she likes to fuss over tiny tots). Equally well-rounded is the *Duende*, matriarchal spirit of the home in Spain and Latin America. Her green

dress echoes her jealous guarding of her adopted home. Russia's *Domovoi* is the soul of a house, and lives behind the stove (his name in Poland derives from a word for "spark.") In some regions he is identified with ancestor spirits, thus raking out the fire at night was a no-no, not just because he requires warmth, but because it represented raking grandfather through the grate into hell. Quite at odds to these industrious, precious guardians is Ireland's *Clurichaun*, cousin of the Leprechaun, who oversees the wine cellar to deter thieves and prevent bottles from corking and otherwise spoiling. Of course, he demands his tribute, since he enjoys a tipple, and you should beware the taste of your dram if he's displeased.

Moral gatekeepers

Brownies are raggedy little house sprites who, as well as zealously looking after the fabric of a home, baking and brewing, washing and sweeping, guard the moral standing of a family. A Brownie is always on the lookout for a thief or glutton, someone who didn't keep her word, who quarreled or erred while working in field, barn, or kitchen. Moreover, this all-seeing, do-gooding spy in the corner, whose ears prick up at the merest thought of a misdeed, can never be bribed. Some fairies live at the threshold (in Scotland under the "door-stane"), to be first to vet visitors and make sure all have returned outside who entered within. This is why in Russia, it is not considered good form to shake hands nor pass packages across a threshold: one must stay out or be invited in.

Welcome these spirits, if not through love, then through fear of what they might inflict once offended. Slighted spirits can't resist curdling milk and burning the supper; indeed they thrive on such disruptive behavior. Russia's *Domovoi*, gets taken by an irresistible urge to tease and pinch, wake the family at night, annoy the cat, throw furniture around, and generally act spitefully. Lithuania's *Kaukas*, if not kept happy, has been known to set the home alight. On March 30, from daybreak till midnight, the *Domovoi* becomes especially manic and wrathful, they say because he is changing his coat, or suffering an intense urge to marry a witch. A good telling off can help.

previous pages 162, 163 and right: **Illustrations from *Elfin Song,* Florence Harrison, 1912, British**
next page: **Roistering elves, Victorian lantern slide**

How to please house spirits

Clean-swept hearth: in Orkney this was to be done every Saturday night, and no one should come near it after.

Warm coals: never rake out the fire before bed; leave the embers glowing. Homes cool quickly at night, and house spirits make use of the fire after you have retired.

Candle stubs: fairies need to be able to see to do their brushing and mending, baking and brewing, and checking of outbuildings, so leave a candle burning at night.

Clean water: plenty of it, left inside the house for bathing. If not, they'll sup on the blood of those who sleep, say people in the Isle of Man. In Russia, house spirits consider the *banya* (communal bathhouse) their own after dark, and a bucket of water and branch of leaves (for whisking the body) should be left for them.

Food and drink: a bowl of the best cream or fresh milk, some good bread, or a bowl of bread in warm milk, even a nice fresh-cooked omelet in Russia, left on the hearth. By taking these offerings, fairies demonstrate their goodwill. On January 28 in Russia, a pot of grain, cooked specially, is left out.

Tiny outfits: in Lithuania one might stitch tiny cloaks for the *Kaukas*, then bury them beneath the cottage floor.

Somewhere to sleep: a cozy crib of hay if they watch outdoors.

Safe retreat: remove all knives and cutting tools from the hearth and cry out before throwing away scalding water, in case the spirit is lurking.

right: **Illustration from *Elfin Song*, Florence Harrison, 1912, British**

Agricultural spirits

Household spirits often extend their watch from hearth and home to field and furrow, preventing sheep and cattle from wandering or theft, protecting stables and barns, helping gather in the harvest, and feeding up favorite beasts, especially among the cattle. (Russia's *Domovoi* is especially fond of cows that match his coloring.) The Swedish *Tomte* is a benevolent farm spirit who rewards only farmers who display good husbandry and kindness to animals. Like household spirits, he requires good food, including a bowl of traditional porridge on Christmas Eve, but many domesticated farm fairies require only the last stalks of grain in a field, and some choice fruit left on branch and vine during harvest, for they gather their life-force from the energy of nature.

Harvest helper

The fairy mill it ground the grain
Nor stayed for anything
And few have seen the fairy folk,
And few have heard them sing.

But when the wet was on the wheat,
And miller-men were dour,
A gnome was toiling through the gloom
To bear them fairy flour.

FLORENCE HARRISON, *THE FAIRY MILL*

left and preceding page: **Illustration from *Elfin Song*, Florence Harrison, 1912, British**
An industrious gnome carries a sack of flour to help out the miller during a bad harvest.

Garden gnomes

Yard spirits have morphed into the garden gnome, who sits guarding the suburban home to bring it good fortune. The first garden gnome, or *Gartenzwerg*, was German, and made from terracotta in the town of Graeferoda in the 1800s. Gnomes become more widely available when mass production began in Germany in the 1870s.

Since the 1960s, factories have spewed out mold-pressed plastic and concrete gnomes, happily fishing, riding pigs, or pushing wheelbarrows, taking a rest on toadstools, wishing wells, or lily pads, pipe in mouth. There is a collector's market for gnomes old and new, with specialist dealers, and craftspeople lovingly hand-painting gnomes from antique molds. One can even buy ironic gnomes topped with the heads of prime ministers and US presidents.

Gnome-napping or abduction has become a crime of urban legend. Gnomes may disappear from a garden for weeks, only to reappear with a fake tan or tiny suitcase. Some send postcards from abroad. Colonies of liberated gnomes congregate in the wild in woods or valleys. Some of this is the work of the Garden Gnome Liberation Front, which has sister organizations in the US, France, Belgium, and Italy. They claim to have the welfare of "captive" gnomes at heart; "Stop Oppressive Gardening" is their slogan. The first European gnome sanctuary for liberated spirits can be found at Barga, Italy. Alternatively, they are smashed or beheaded to set free their spirits.

left: **A cheerful garden gnome with his friendly lantern**
These miniature fellows trace their origins back to ancient folklore.

Fairy godmother

The fairy godmother has launched a thousand gown-hire stores and matriarchal dating agencies. Related to the fate fairies who visit a baby shortly after birth to determine her future, fairy godmothers emerge relatively late, in the French salon fairy-tale tradition (whose tellers, like their fairy characters, were wise older women). She is best known in versions of the Cinderella story as a protective spirit who grants wishes to those who have need of her, usually young women.

Her power is not only expressed in enchantment—conjuring dresses out of air, carriages from pumpkins, and staff from mice—but in offering advice; wisdom accrued through years of experience, for she knows the ways of the world (don't stay out with a strange man after midnight). This good mother epitomizes the ideals of motherhood: wisdom, love, and boundless resources. In the Perrault tale *The Fairy,* the spirit of the title is not an all-forgiving mother, but one who bestows riches only on those who merit it. She tests her protégées by dressing as an old woman (á la Disney's Cinderella), who deserves courtesy, respect, and help, and whose supernatural rewards, or punishments, reflect the treatment she receives.

left **Cinderalla and her fairy godmother, Edmund Dulac, *The Sleeping Beauty and Other Tales From the Old French,* 1910, French**
Cinderalla watches as her fairy godmother points her wand to the finest pumpkin to transform it into a coach.

Toads and diamonds

There was once upon a time a widow who had two daughters. The eldest was so much like her in the face and humor that whoever looked upon the daughter saw the mother. They were both so disagreeable and so proud that there was no living with them.

The youngest, who was the very picture of her father for courtesy and sweetness and humor, was withal one of the most beautiful girls ever seen. As people naturally love their own likeness, this mother even doted on her eldest daughter, and at the same time had a horrible aversion for the youngest–she made her eat in the kitchen and work continually. Among other things, this poor child was forced twice a day to draw water above a mile and a half away from the house and bring home a pitcherful of it. One day as she was at this fountain there came to her a poor woman, who begged of her to let her drink.

"Oh! ay, with all my heart, Goody," said this pretty little girl; and rinsing immediately the pitcher, she took up some water from the clearest place of the fountain and gave it to her, holding up the pitcher all the while, that she might drink the easier.

The good woman having drunk said to her:

"You are so very pretty, my dear, so good and mannerly, that I cannot help giving you a gift." For this was a fairy who had taken the form of a poor country woman to see how far the civility and good manners of this pretty girl would go. "I would give you for a gift," continued the fairy, "that every word you speak there shall come out of your mouth either a flower or a jewel."

When this pretty girl came home her mother scolded at her for staying so long at the fountain.

"I beg your pardon, mamma," said the poor girl, for not making more haste." And in speaking these words there came out of her mouth two roses, two pearls, and two diamonds.

"What is it I see there?" said her mother, quite astonished. "I think I see diamonds and pearls come out of this girl's mouth! How happens this, child?"

This was the first time she had ever called her child.

The poor creature told her frankly all the matter, not without dropping out infinite numbers of diamonds.

"In good faith," cried the mother, "I must send my child thither. Come hither, Fanny. Look what comes out of thy sister's mouth when she speaks. Wouldst not thou be glad, my dear, to have the same gift given to thee? Thou hast nothing else to do but go and draw water out of the fountain, and when a certain poor woman asks you to let her drink to give it to her very civilly."

"It would be a very fine sight indeed," said this ill-bred minx, "to see me go draw water."

"You shall go, hussy!" said the mother, "and this minute." So away she went, but grumbling all the way, taking with her the best silver tankard in the house. She was no sooner at the fountain than she saw coming out of the wood a lady most gloriously dressed who came up to her and asked to drink. This was, you must know, the very fairy who appeared to her sister, but had now taken the air and dress of a princess, to see how far this girl's rudeness would go.

ladyship, was it? However, you may drink out of it, if you have a fancy."

"You are not over and above mannerly," answered the fairy, without putting herself in a passion. "Well, then, since you have so little breeding and are so disobliging, I give you for gift that every word you speak there shall come out of your mouth a snake or a toad."

So soon as her mother saw her coming she cried out:

"Well, daughter?" "Well, mother?" answered the pert hussy, throwing out of her mouth two vipers and two toads.

"Oh! mercy," cried the mother; "what is it I see? Oh! it is that wretch her sister who has occasioned all this; but she shall pay for it." And immediately she ran to beat her. The poor child fled away from her and went to hide herself in the forest not far from thence.

The king's son, then on his return from hunting, met her, and seeing her so very pretty, asked her what she did there alone and why she cried. "Alas! sir, my mamma has turned me out of doors."

The king's son, who saw five or six pearls and as many diamonds come out of her mouth, desired her to tell him how that happened. She thereupon told him the whole story; and so the king's son fell in love with her, and considering himself that such a gift was worth more than any marriage portion, conducted her to the palace of the king his father and there married her. As for her sister, she made herself so much hated that her own mother turned her off and the miserable wretch, having wandered about a good while without finding anybody to take her in, went to a corner of the wood and there died.

ANDREW LANG, *THE BLUE FAIRY BOOK*

above: **Illustration from *Elfin Song*, Florence Harrison, 1912, British**

Those that see the people of Faerie
most often, and so have the most
of their wisdom, are often very
poor, but often, too, they are
thought to have a strength
beyond man …

W.B. YEATS

It is the season now to go
About the country high and low,
Among the lilacs hand in hand,
And two by two in fairy land.

ROBERT LOUIS STEVENSON

If ye will with Mab find grace,
Set each platter in his place;
Rake the fire up, and get
Water in, ere sun be set.
Wash your pails and cleanse your dairies,
Sluts are loathsome to the fairies;
Sweep your house; Who doth not so,
Mab will pinch her by the toe.

ROBERT HERRICK

chapter 5
Mischievous Work

I am that merry wanderer of the night.
I jest to Oberon, and make him smile
When I a fat and bean-fed horse beguile,
Neighing in likeness of a filly foal;
And sometime lurk I in a gossip's bowl
In very likeness of a roasted crab,
And when she drinks, against her lips I bob
And on her withered dewlap pour the ale.
The wisest aunt, telling the saddest tale,
Sometime for three-foot stool mistaketh me;
Then slip I from her bum, down topples she,
And 'tailor' cries, and falls into a cough;
And then the whole quire hold their hips and laugh,
And waxen in their mirth, and neeze, and swear
A merrier hour was never wasted there.

WILLIAM SHAKESPEARE, *A MIDSUMMER NIGHT'S DREAM*

previous page: **Puck and a fairy, Arthur Rackham, from** *Shakespeare's A Midsummer Night's Dream,* **first published 1908, British**
Puck prepares for a night of mischief.
right: **Puck/Robin Goodfellow, Arthur Rackham, from** *Shakespeare's A Midsummer Night's Dream,* **first published 1908, British**
Shakespeare's amoral sprite delights in playing pranks.

Joyce Plumstead

Mischief-making sprites

While not actively malicious, like the shape-sifting demons intent on luring mortals to a grisly end, a host of quick-witted tricksters have great fun at the expense of humankind. Theirs is a benevolent, if subversive type of disorder that bends the laws of physics, challenges the established rule, and pushes at the boundaries of human reason. These creatures tend to live alongside us in the mortal world; they may even be those same spirits who industriously help care for home and land.

Defined by manic disembodied laughter, these irrepressible tricksters revel in the chaos that ensues when they steal horses to ride at dead of night, hide vital tools, and lead men astray by conjuring paths—a phenomenon known as being pixie-led.

… mischief everywhere
The maids, to keep the elves aloof,
will bar the doors in vain,
No keyhole will be fairy proof …

THOMAS HAYNES BAYLY, *FAIRY SONG*

left: **A naughty imp, Joyce Plumstead from *Holiday Stories*, *1936*, British**
It's hard to stop this mischievous sprite from getting up to his tricks.

Humankind tries to adapt everyday life to accommodate the mischief, maneuvering around it rather than actively tackling it. Sometimes the behavior of human beings determines whether elves and their companions make merry mischief or create total havoc. In the north of England a house Brownie neglected by his family—perhaps they forgot to leave out some cream or donate a portion of the supper dish—might metamorphose into a Boggart, famed for causing accidents, taunting, and teasing. It is our own fears that decide the tricks played and the ensuing fright: North American stories of being fairy-led are particularly resonant, as befits those facing a new life in a strange, vast wilderness, where people you follow may well be unknown. Tricky characters come in all shapes and sizes.

Elves: German, British, Icelandic, and Scandinavian elves, like the *Alfs* of Viking legend, live alongside us and though they can be industrious stitchers and shoe-makers, they can't resist tangling hair while people and animals sleep (elf-lock), thinking up birthmarks for the unborn (elf marks), and deforming vegetables as they grow (elf-twisting), as well as the usual pilfering and generalized mayhem. Russia's household *Domovoi* also enjoys mussing hair: beards and horses manes are his thing. He has been known secretly to braid women's hair, though when he's in a good mood he makes a good job of it.

Pixies: On Britain's southwest fringe, especially in Cornwall, where they are known as piskeys, these elf-like sprites delight in capriciousness. In the home they fling objects around a room if displeased. Outdoors, they ride horses so recklessly at night that they are fit for nothing by morning, as are unwary travelers lead astray by their bobbing lanterns.

Leprechauns: Though diligent at shoemaking, these Irish spirits are tricksy, and thrive on human greed. They will promise to reveal the crock of gold each guards, but inevitably hoodwink the gullible mortal, disappearing to echoes of laughter.

Boggarts: These shape-shifting household spirits of northern England are provoked into mischief and pranks by their human companions. They might disturb the bedclothes, shake the curtains, slam doors, or upset the cooking pans. By night, they have been known to lurk outdoors by hills, waiting to chase and frighten travelers.

Kobold: Germany's household *Kobold* is happy to scour pans and fatten up horses, but is prone to bouts of vengeful acts (beating up the servants) if he doesn't get served on time with his sweetened milk. A *Kobold* in the household of the Bishop of Hildesheim strangled one servant and threw another in the moat.

Trasgues: In Asturias, Spain, the ugly little *Trasgu* works happily around home and orchard by night, but, as with all these spirits, once displeased, goes crazy. (It can be enough that the chores are finished before bedtime). But he is not actively malign to humans, like his fellow spirit the *Malino*, who hides in foodstuffs and water ready to enter the bodies of the unwary and cause mysterious illness.

Nisse: These little packages of trouble work diligently around home and farm, like the Swedish *Tomte*, to a point. Once slighted, they do everything possible to be revenged, using the wiles of a Boggart. They might steal from neighboring homes to stir up trouble.

There was a Nis in Jutland who was very much teased by a mischievous boy. When the Nis had done his work he sat down to have his supper, and he found that the boy had been playing tricks with his porridge and made it unpleasant. So he made up his mind to be revenged, and he did it in this way. The boy slept with a servant-man in the loft. The Nis went up to them and took off the bed-clothes. Then, looking at the little boy lying beside the tall man, he said, "Long and short don't match," and he took the boy by the legs and pulled him down to the man's legs. This was not to his mind, however, so he went to the head of the bed and looked at them, Then said the Nis-"Short and long don't match," and he pulled the boy up again; and so he went on all through the night, up and down, down and up, till the boy was punished enough.

JOHN THACKRAY BUNCE, *FAIRY TALES; THEIR ORIGIN AND MEANING WITH SOME ACCOUNT OF DWELLERS IN FAIRYLAND*

right: **Ruined porridge, Joyce Plumstead from *Holiday Stories*, 1936, British**
The Nis fairy is well-known for getting into the porridge pot.

Puck's work

Much less malicious than their cousins, the goblins, who can be quite terrifying, Hobgoblins enjoy practical, sometimes spiteful, jokes around home and wayside. In *A Midsummer Night's Dream,* Shakespeare characterized the Hobgoblin in Puck, "that shrewd and knavish sprite" also known as Robin Goodfellow (or Rob-goblin).

Once of Puck's preferred pranks is to lurk in bushes, wells, or hills on a long winter's night, making familiar voices, and maybe carrying a lantern or becoming a Will-o-the-wisp to lead wanderers through "mire and clay." He abandons them to their fate in the middle of a bog or atop a cliff, with a peal of excited laughter. "Ho, ho, ho!" was Puck's trademark long before it was purloined by Santa—and expressed not contentment, but wicked enjoyment of others' misfortune. Those who find themselves lost on a dark night might still be told "Robin Goodfellow has been with you tonight," as they have since the sixteenth century.

left: **Robin Goodfellow, Charles Folkard, from *The Children's Shakespeare,* 1911, British**

In this enticing guise Robin Goodfellow leads travelers astray in the dark.

Puck is the archetypal trickster of English fairy lore, and an crucial central character in ballads and broadsides, plays, and novels. Although, like Robin Hood, with whom he has been linked, Puck looks after the poor and needy, and is particularly fond of lovers, he can't stop himself from playing tricks, primarily shape-shifting exploits involving leading people astray, terrifying, and pinching. He can't resist an easy target, such as the very young, the very old, and those who are sleeping. Yet because tricksters are by nature contradictory, he is known also for helping around the house, Brownie-style, in exchange for a bowl of cream or curds. In parts of Ireland, his cousin, Pooka, when he appears in humanoid form, may also work in home and field, demanding "Pooka's share" of the harvest, or suitable gifts left at the hill from which he emerges.

As a shape-shifter extraordinaire, Puck the free spirit flits between forms, shown in the startling variety of descriptions of him, and names (there are versions in various Scandinavian and German languages, and in Latvian and Lithuanian, too). Is he a deformed goblin, a capricious elf, or a hairy fairy? An animal with goat's feet, an eagle, or a coltish horse? Shakespeare even describes Puck inhabiting drinking cups and stools, ready to unsettle their users. The "terrible steed" is one of his favorite forms, as it is of his fearsome Irish cousin, Pooka. In this disguise he tempts humans to mount him, then canters excitedly over many a terrifying mile, often depositing the exhausted rider in a ditch or over a precipice. His awesome reputation spread to animals: the very sight of the spirit can cause them to stop laying or giving milk!

right: Warwick Goble, *The Book of Fairy Poetry,* 1920, British
A hostile woodland spirit threatens human interlopers.

Fierce border guardians

Boundary places are a particular worry for travelers because of the mischievous, or downright malevolent, spirits that guard them. The trolls of Scandinavian fairytales may be found at crossings points, lurking beneath bridges, ready to abduct—or eat—unsuspecting travelers. They may be placated by offerings or by guile, as in the tale *The Three Billy-Goats Gruff*. What such tales suggest is that though mankind and supernaturals inhabit different realms, at some points the two worlds intersect, making meetings unavoidable, and correct behavior vital. At borders patrolled by folks from the other world you should greet fairies politely with a "Good day and good luck to you little people," say those who believe in the Isle of Man. Give them a wide berth, and they might not impede your progress.

The Three Billy-Goats Gruff

Once on a time there were three Billy-goats, who were to go up to the hill-side to make themselves fat, and the name of all three was "Gruff." On the way up was a bridge over a burn they had to cross; and under the bridge lived a great ugly Troll, with eyes as big as saucers, and a nose as long as a poker.

So first of all came the youngest billy-goat Gruff to cross the bridge.

"Trip, trap! trip, trap!" went the bridge.

"WHO'S THAT tripping over my bridge?" roared the Troll.

"Oh, it is only I, the tiniest billy-goat Gruff; and I'm going up to the hill-side to make myself fat," said the billy-goat, with such a small voice.

"Now, I'm coming, to gobble you up," said the Troll.

"Oh, no! pray don't take me. I'm too little, that I am," said the billy-goat; "wait a bit till the second billy-goat Gruff comes, he's much bigger."

"Well, be off with you;" said the Troll.

A little while after came the second billy-goat Gruff to cross the bridge.

"TRIP, TRAP! TRIP, TRAP! TRIP, TRAP!" went the bridge.

"WHO'S THAT tripping over my bridge?" roared the Troll.

"Oh, it's the second billy-goat Gruff, and I'm going up to the hill-side to make myself fat," said the billy-goat, who hadn't such a small voice.

"Now I'm coming to gobble you up," said the Troll.

"Oh, no! don't take me, wait a little till the big billy-goat Gruff comes, he's much bigger."

"Very well! be off with you," said the Troll.

But just then up came the big billy-goat Gruff.

"TRIP, TRAP! TRIP, TRAP! TRIP, TRAP!" went the bridge, for the billy-goat was so heavy that the bridge creaked and groaned under him.

"WHO'S THAT tramping over my bridge?" roared the Troll.

"IT'S I! THE BIG BILLY-GOAT GRUFF," said the billy-goat, who had an ugly hoarse voice of his own.

"Now I'm coming to gobble you up," roared the Troll,

"Well, come along! I've got two spears,
And I'll poke your eyeballs out at your ears;
I've got besides two curling-stones,
And I'll crush you to bits, body and bones."

That was what the big billy-goat said; and so he flew at the Troll, and poked his eyes out with his horns, and crushed him to bits, body and bones, and tossed him out into the burn, and after that he went up to the hill-side. There the billy-goats got so fat they were scarce able to walk home again; and if the fat hasn't fallen off them, why, they're still fat; and so-

"Snip, snap, snout
This tale's told out."

GEORGE WEBBE DASENT. *EAST O' THE SUN AND WEST O' THE MOON*

Seductive spirits

Mischief-making fairies come no more dangerous than those that take the form of alluring spirits who entrap mortals by arousing love or lustful thoughts. These human-sized figures are eerily beautiful and emerge from territories where humans cannot thrive: deep in the woods, beneath the waves. One kiss is enough to grip a heart or unravel a mortal mind. Even mere devotees of fairy poetry and painting are caught up in the unearthly beauty, flushing as the poet or painter rushes to embrace the theme. In Yeats' words "Our cheeks are pale, our hair is unbound, our breasts are heaving, our eyes are agleam."

But these spirits only suck our life-blood warm the tales, like the stunningly beautiful Manx fairy muse, *Lhiannan-shee*, who attaches herself to poets and musicians, inspiring them to ever greater feats of creation, while slowly inhaling energy from their shells. As she casts aside the first fey young man, she readies herself to devour another.

Seductive spirits of the nether regions of the world, Mermaids sun themselves at the ocean's edge, singing irresistible songs to draw the sailors who lust after them into the merciless surf, or brewing storms to punish those who forsake them. The wary might gain a clue to the Mermaid's deceitful nature by the mirror she carries, which suggests multiplicity, or by that impenetrable tail. Though she oozes temptation, she can only stay virginal.

right: *Full Fathom Five,* Edmund Dulac, from Shakespeare's *Comedy of the Tempest*, 1908
Dulac's gorgeous sirens lure their victims to a watery grave.

Fatal attraction

"Buy from us with a golden curl."
She clipped a precious golden lock,
She dropped a tear more rare than pearl,
Then sucked their fruit globes fair or red:
Sweeter than honey from the rock,
Stronger than man-rejoicing wine,
Clearer than water flowed that juice;
She never tasted such before,
How should it cloy with length of use?
She sucked and sucked and sucked the more
Fruits which that unknown orchard bore,
She sucked until her lips were sore;
Then flung the emptied rinds away,
But gathered up one kernel stone,
And knew not was it night or day
As she turned home alone.

CHRISTINA ROSSETTI, *GOBLIN MARKET*

left: **Illustration by Warwick Goble from *The Book of Fairy Poetry*,
1920, British**
Fairy fruits prove overwhelmingly tempting but ultimately unsatisfying.

It isn't only men who should be wary of enchantment. In Christina Rossetti's poem, *Goblin Market,* it is not the seductive nature of the goblin men, so much as her desire to *be* seduced that leads the human female into temptation. On the other hand, the *Gan Ceanach,* or love talker, is a real smoothie, whispering sweetnesses into ears ready to swoon. The maidens he mesmerizes pine away once he moves on, as, of course, he does. Mer and Selkie men may take human lovers, who are fated to live as single mothers. More malignly, the elfin knight of Scottish ballads seduces virgins by supernatural means and leaves them not satisfied in the marital bed, but lifeless on the river bed.

But it is men who are most at risk of seduction. Wood-wives of northern Europe, mistresses of this game, entice unwary but game herds- and huntsmen from their tasks and families. In Brittany she takes the form of the dazzlingly beautiful Korrigan temptress, who sits in the gloom of the forest canopy (light disagrees with her complexion) near a ruined well, combing and braiding her flaxen hair with golden pins. Fairy-pin wells are places of pilgrimage still in Britain.

As her victim approaches she flushes with passion, her star-bright eyes tinge red, and with a flash of her wand, the well becomes a stately château, with tapestry-covered walls, dazzling lights, tableware, velvet couches, music of flutes and viols, and attendant maidens to wait on the entrapped bridegroom. As with all fairy temptresses and palaces, all is all moss and leaves. In one tale, the charm dissolves with the first ray of daylight "and the Korrigan became a hideous hag, as repulsive as before she had been lovely; the walls of her palace and the magnificence which had furnished it, became once more tree and thicket, its carpets moss, its tapestries leaves, its silver cups wild roses, and its dazzling mirrors pools of stagnant water."

Charmed to death

One of Keats' most famous poems, *La Belle Dame sans Merci,* is a chilling account of the fate of a young man who falls under the fatal spell of a beautiful fairy lover.

Full beautiful–a faery's child,
Her hair was long, her foot was light,
And her eyes were wild.

I made a garland for her head,
And bracelets too, and fragrant zone;
She look'd at me as she did love,
And made sweet moan.

I set her on my pacing steed,
And nothing else saw all day long,
For sidelong would she bend, and sing
A faery's song.

She found me roots of relish sweet,
And honey wild, and manna dew,
And sure in language strange she said–
"I love thee true."

She took me to her elfin grot,
And there she wept, and sigh'd fill sore,
And there I shut her wild wild eyes
With kisses four.
And there she lulled me asleep,
And there I dream'd—Ah! woe betide!
The latest dream I ever dream'd
On the cold hill's side.

I saw pale kings and princes too,
Pale warriors, death-pale were they all;
They cried-"La Belle Dame sans Merci
Hath thee in thrall!"

I saw their starved lips in the gloam,
With horrid warning gaped wide,
And I awoke and found me here,
On the cold hill's side.

And this is why I sojourn here,
Alone and palely loitering,
Though the sedge is wither'd from the lake,
And no birds sing.

JOHN KEATS, *LA BELLE DAME SANS MERCI*

above: **Illustration by Warwick Goble from *The Book of Fairy Poetry*,** **1920, British**

The thirteenth fairy

The vengeful fairy is most popularly portrayed in the tale of *Sleeping Beauty,* or *Briar Rose,* in which a king and queen "accidentally" forget to invite the thirteenth fairy to the celebration of their child's birth (they only have twelve diamond-encrusted place settings). Her twelve fairy sisters graciously attend, bearing all the blessings a young girl could desire— beauty, wit, grace, the ability to dance, sing, and play—only to have them all undone by the wronged fairy, who crashes the event.

Thirteen is a magical number, which has come to be associated with chaos, forces outside human control, and bad fortune. Since it exploded in popularity in the nineteenth century across Europe and North America, this superstition, which claims roots in everything from Norse myth and moon worship to the Bible, has driven the number 13, like a bad fairy, out of street and storey numbering. Only in Italy does the number remain intact, associated with Christ and his twelve disciples.

right: **The 13th fairy, Willy Planck in *Deutsches Marchenbuch,* 'Dornroschen,' 1870–1956**
The power of the thirteenth fairy is derived from the force of vengeance which brings bad luck and chaos to human beings.
next page: **Illustration from *Elfin Song,* Florence Harrison, 1912, British**

Little Briar Rose

A long time ago there were a king and queen who said every day, "Ah, if only we had a child," but they never had one.

But it happened that once when the queen was bathing, a frog crept out of the water on to the land, and said to her, "Your wish shall be fulfilled, before a year has gone by, you shall have a daughter."

What the frog had said came true, and the queen had a little girl who was so pretty that the king could not contain himself for joy, and ordered a great feast. He invited not only his kindred, friends and acquaintances, but also the wise women, in order that they might be kind and well-disposed towards the child. There were thirteen of them in his kingdom, but, as he had only twelve golden plates for them to eat out of, one of them had to be left at home.

The feast was held with all manner of splendor and when it came to an end the wise women bestowed their magic gifts upon the baby - one gave virtue, another beauty, a third riches, and so on with everything in the world that one can wish for.

When eleven of them had made their promises, suddenly the thirteenth came in. She wished to avenge herself for not having been invited, and without greeting, or even looking at anyone, she cried with a loud voice, "The king's daughter shall in her fifteenth year prick herself with a spindle, and fall down dead." And, without saying a word more, she turned round and left the room.

They were all shocked, but the twelfth, whose good wish still remained unspoken, came forward, and as she could not undo the evil sentence, but only soften it, she said, it shall not be death, but a deep sleep of a hundred years, into which the princess shall fall.

JACOB AND WILHELM GRIMM, *HOUSEHOLD TALES*

Fairy thieving

It is true that some fairies have a reputation for being light-fingered, but in many cases, it is because we human beings are being careless or lazy, and the fairies take a golden opportunity to both help themselves and punish erring mortals at the same time. Take Lazy Liza in Florence Harrison's poem of that name. She *knew* that the apples on her tree were ripe for picking, but she was just too lazy to get up and harvest them. Until it was too late! The fairies got them instead:

Lazy Liza cried: "Alack!"
  Woe the fairies!
Will they bring my apples back
  To the windy trees?"
"Nay," the linnet said, "and Nay,"
"Fruit the fairies steal away
  Never comes again."

FLORENCE HARRISON, *ELFIN SONG*

right: **Illustration from *Elfin Song,* Florence Harrison, 1912, British**
Stolen fruits always taste sweeter.

Give me your peas!

Marigold Mary, shelling peas
  "Give me a dozen," the Kobold said.
"Only a dozen, a dozen, please,
A dozen peas for my flower bed."

Marigold Mary's hair was gold,
  Her hair was long, but it stood upright,
Till she looked, to that old and bald Kobold,
  Like a torch alight on a windy night.

She dropped her peas and away she ran,
  Away and out in the twilight grey.
"I'm glad she did," said the Fairy Man,
  As he gathered her peas and walked away.

FLORENCE HARRISON, *ELFIN SONG*

left: **Illustration from *Elfin Song*, Florence Harrison, 1912, British**
Mary is terrified into giving away her precious peas .

A pinch and a punch

Pinch him, pinch him, blacke and blue,
Sawcie mortalls must not view
What the Queene of Stars is doing,
Nor pry into our Fairy wooing.

JOHN LYLY, *ENDIMION*

Misname or bad talk, pry into fairy affairs, leave less than the best cream by the hearth: you'll regret it, as these are ways to vex the fay and provoke them into action. Some fairies carry particular chips on their shoulders: take the Manx *Adhene*, or "themselves," a name humans must get right and never take in vain.

If offended, some spirits can cause illness in the humans who have aggravated them, or in their beasts. Tribes of disease demons stalk many mythologies. Others just nip the flesh until black and blue, a traditional English form of fairy come-uppance, best carried out at night or while invisible and accompanied by a fiery buzzing. In some cases, the pinching causes a victim to fall into an entranced sleep. This is a popular form of punishment for those who set out to spy on the fairies at work or revels, and for those who try to capture them.

right: Illustration by Warwick Goble from *The Book of Fairy Poetry*, 1920, British

Whir! whir! whir! as if a flight of bees were passing him, buzzed in his ears. Every limb, from head to foot, was as if stuck full of pins and pinched with tweezers. He could not move, he was changed to the ground. By some means he had rolled down the mound, and lay on his back with his arms outstretched, arms and legs being secured by magic chains to the earth; therefore, although he suffered great agony, he could not stir, and, strange enough, his tongue appeared tied by cords, so that he could not call. He had lain, no one can tell how long, in this sad plight, when he felt as if a number of insects were running over him, and by the light of the moon he saw standing on his nose one of the spriggans, who looked exceedingly like a small dragon-fly. This little monster stamped and jumped with great delight; and having had his own fun upon the elevated piece of humanity, he laughed most outrageously, and shouted, "Away, away, I smell the day!" Upon this the army of small people, who had taken possession of the old man's body, moved quickly away, and left our discomfited hero alone on the Gump. Bewildered, or, as he said, bedeviled, he lay still to gather up his thoughts. At length the sun arose, and then he found that he had been tied to the ground by myriads of gossamer webs, which were now covered with dew, and glistened like diamonds in the sunshine.

ROBERT HUN, *POPULAR ROMANCES OF THE WEST OF ENGLAND*

Elves on the warpath

There every herd, by sad experience, knows
How, winged with fate, their elf-shot arrows fly,
When the sick ewe her summer food forgoes,
Or, stretched on earth, the heart-smit heifers lie.

WILLIAM COLLINS, *ODE ON THE POPULAR SUPERSTITIONS*
OF THE HIGHLANDS OF SCOTLAND

Mischievous fairies are prone to attack livestock with tiny triangular flint darts, causing sudden cramps and seizures, a phenomenon known as "elf-shot." If the animal does not die but remains paralyzed, it is thought that its soul and substance have been transported to fairyland, and a shell or replica left to die. One theory has it that the arrows (sometimes invisible) came from a troll, who shattered to a thousand flints. Other that the arrows were shot from gold-tipped bows formed from human ribs or fairy breast-pins, sourced from Mermaids. Archaeologists state that elf-arrows or fairy shot are, in fact, Neolithic arrowheads.

Elf stroke is a similar paralysis affecting mortals, said to be caused by a malicious fairy's blow of the hand. In Newfoundland, fairy blast results in a wound that may become a tumor. Urban legends abound of surgeons dissecting tumors to discover fairy peculiarities within, including pins and teeth, feathers and hair. In Scandinavia, the breath of an elf on the skin could cause *älvablåst* (elf blast or elf wind): blisters or rashes or even paralysis. Remedies include a counterblow: a blast of the bellows or a brisk rubbing with pages from the Bible.

Those bolts are of various sizes, of a hard yellowish substance, resembling somewhat the flint, for which they are no bad substitutes. The bolt is very frequently of the shape of a heart, its edges being indented like a saw, and very sharp at the point. This deadly weapon the wicked fairy will throw at man or beast with such precision as seldom to miss his aim, and whenever it hits, the stroke is fatal. Such is the great force with which it is flung, that on its striking the object, it instantaneously perforates it to the heart, and a sudden death is the consequence. In the blinking of an eye, a man or an ox is struck down cold dead, and, strange to say, the wound is not discernible to an ordinary person.

W. GRANT STEWART, *THE POPULAR SUPERSTITIONS AND FESTIVE AMUSEMENTS OF THE HIGHLANDERS OF SCOTLAND*

left: **Illustration from *Elfin Song,* Florence Harrison, 1912, British**
A fairy sallies forth armed with a tiny but sharply pointed spear.

Things that go bump in the night

Because fairies are beings of the night, much of their mischief is carried out during the hours of darkness, while mortals lie sleeping. It is not surprising, then, that they are linked in many traditions, with sleep disorders. In German lore, it is elves who cause bad dreams: *Albtraum* translates as "elf-dream," in Japan it is *Baku*, eater of dreams. There are ranks of spirits who enjoy messing with children's dreams, too: the *Painajainen* of the Alpine region among them, who appear as tiny white horses. Russia's homey *Domovoi* is thought to interfere with breathing as people sleep, and to stir up nightmares.

In many cultures a victim wakes suddenly breathless and paralyzed to see a crouched figure squatting on the chest. In Newfoundland it is called being "hag-ridden" for the sprite who appears; in Japan it is experiencing *kanashibari* and often brings a white-clad figure. The vision is pictured vividly in Henry Fuseli's iconic and highly charged Gothic painting of 1871, "The Nightmare." The Teutonic *Mara*, or crusher spirit, namer of the nightmare and *cauchemar*, and bringer of the experience, is pictured as the mare at the back of the painting, and is connected with the incubus (male) and sucubus (female) spirits who incapacitate, assault, and rape the sleeping, invisibly, as a beast, or in human guise.

right: Leal da Camara, *L'assiette au beurre,* 1903, French
A diabolical nightmare spirit hovers over an unfortunate victim's bed.

The green fairy

The first stage is like ordinary drinking, the second when you begin to see monstrous and cruel things, but if you can persevere you will enter in upon the third stage where you see … wonderful curious things.

OSCAR WILDE

The legendary green fairy is not a mischievous spirit in human form with wings, but a seductively intoxicating spirit that gives the mind wings, for absinthe, the famed hallucinatory drink, gained the nickname *la fée verte,* or green fairy, for its intense color and mind-bending effects. You might remember her as the sprite in a wisp of green played by Kylie Minogue in Baz Luhrmann's movie, *Moulin Rouge.*

The naughty spirit was concocted in the late eighteenth century in Switzerland as a panacea, and first mass-distilled by Henri-Louis Pernod in the early 1800s. Its mystical associations begin with a key ingredient, *Artemesia absinthium* (wormwood), one of the most important fairy ointment plants. Its constituent thujone has psychoactive properties. Other magic herbs in the mix included hallucinogenic nutmeg, calamus, also thought psychoactive, anise, said to give an opium-like high, lemon balm to "chase away melancholy," and the seizure-causing sedative hyssop. Its constituents fennel and juniper protect against bad spirits.

left: **Poster by Privat Liremont, in *Les Affiches Etrangeres,* 1897, French**

Hark! is that a horn I hear,
In cloudland winding sweet –
And bell-like clash of bridle-rein,
And silver-shod light feet?
Is it the elfin laughter
Of fairies riding faint and high,
Beneath the branches of the moon,
Straying through the starry sky?

WALTER DE LA MARE

Benighted travellers now lose their way
    whom the Will-of-the-wisp bewitches
About and about he leads them astray
    Through bogs, through hedges, and ditches

SIR WILLIAM DAVENANT

I am gone, gone far, with the fairies roaming,
You may ask of me where the herons are
In the open marsh when the snipe are homing,
Or when no moon lights nor a single star.
On stormy nights when the streams are foaming
And a hint may come of my haunts afar,
With the reeds my floor and my roof the
   gloaming,
But I come no more to Ballynar.

LORD DUNSANAY

chapter 6

Powers of Enchantment

The fairy ring

Dare you haunt our hallow'd green?
None but fairies here are seen.
Down and sleep,
Wake and weep,
Pinch him black, and pinch him blue,
That seeks to steal a lover true!
When you come to hear us sing,
Or to tread our fairy ring,
Pinch him black, and pinch him blue!
O thus our nails shall handle you!

THOMAS RAVENSCROFT

previous page: **Fairy and water baby, Warwick Goble from Charles Kingsley's _The Water Babies,_ 1910, British**
right: **How the fairy ring is made, Arthur Rackham, Shakespeare's _The Tempest,_ 1928, British**

The lure of the dance

The ring of dance haunts many a fairy tale, a means of drawing mortals into the warped time and space of fairyland. Fairies and elves cavort at night or before dawn on misty mornings. Join the circling dancers at your peril: once entranced, few make it home. Because a ring has neither beginning nor end, it is all but impossible to break from. Not only is the ring dance magical, so too are the marks it leaves. The tireless tripping of tiny feet etches a circle motif into the ground; it can appear as deep green tufts or a scorched effect. The grass within may look lusher, dry as thatch, or even reddish in hue—in Orkney it shows as a ring of green on bare heathland—and at certain times of year, a ring of mushrooms sprouts from it. The size of a fairy ring varies, from a few inches to 200 feet (60 meters) or more in diameter. Fairy rings are extremely slow-growing—it is thought that some larger examples are hundreds of years old. Not only is the ring perilous for humans to step within, its grass is unpalatable for grazing animals, who are intuitive to its danger signals. Except for Welsh sheep. The superior quality of Welsh mutton is credited to those reckless sheep greedily munching on the grass of the fairy ring!

One might be drawn to the ring by fairy music. Fatally charming for human ears, it weaves dreams and acts as a sleeping draft or love potion. You will never have a better time, the tales tell, and never weary. But when you stop dancing, or are pulled away by a loved one who remains bravely with one foot outside the ring, you may find a year and a day—or a lifetime—has passed. Some drop dead from exhaustion. Those who do return are described as dulled or befuddled, moving trance-like through life, unable to recall the tune, the dance or partner, but also unable to forget.

One day a gentleman entered a cabin in the County Clare, and saw a young girl about twenty seated by the fire, chanting a melancholy song, without settled words or music. On inquiry he was told she had once heard the fairy harp, and those who hear it lose all memory of love or hate, and forget all things, and never more have any other sound in their ears save the soft music of the fairy harp, and when the spell is broken, they die.

LADY WILDE, *ANCIENT LEGENDS, MYSTIC CHARMS, AND SUPERSTITIONS OF IRELAND*

next page: **Fairy rings and toadstools, Richard Doyle, 1875, British** Moonlight ring dances around the toadstools.

Magic mushrooms

One of the prime signifiers of anything fairy is a creature sitting on a Fly Agaric mushroom, the toadstool; its red and white spots shout "supernatural," like the iconic red outfits of many wee folk. In some traditions fairies feed on these strange fungal foodstuffs, that are, at turns, delicious and deadly. Many bear fairy names: Fairies' Bonnets, Fairy Cake, Elf Cup, Pixie Cap. The names Dryad's Saddle and Fly Agaric hint that mushrooms offer a way for the earthbound to fly: "magic" mushrooms have hallucinogenic properties; you can take a trip on them. Ethno-mycologists trace the association of hallucinogenic plants with the spirit world back to the Paleolithic period.

left: **Fairy revels, Mildred Entwhistle, from *Allers Familj Journal*, 1927**
A toadstool makes a fun merry-go-round.

The power of invisibility

Fairies like to be clandestine, so what better way of moving around bustling human markets and towns than to be invisible? Invisibility is one reason why the little people are so feared by mankind: one never knows where they are and what they might over-hear, which is why it is important to use euphemisms when speaking of them. All you might know of their presence is a jingling of invisible bridles, a rustle of duchesse satin, a scent, or the notes of an unsettling air on the wind. The only evidence of a fairy visit might be the loss of a favorite drinking vessel, disturbed sheets, or a space in the cradle.

Fairies are skilled at camouflage, and by their attire and movements are able to disguise themselves as lichen, a sapling, a butterfly, or fish. Sometimes a fairy might be visible to one protagonist in a story (often to a child), but invisible to companions. A cloak or cap is often the source of invisibility, or hints at other supernatural powers (foxglove bonnets pay homage to a powerful herbal remedy, and the antlers worn by the Manitou nod at the ceremonial magic of the Algonquin people.)

The Grimm Brothers say that we don't usually see dwarves—not because they live below ground, but because, when abroad, they generally sport protective, invisible-making "fog hats." The Irish Merrow don a small red-feathered cap that proffers an ability to live beneath the waves. Removing the magical cap on land is a perilous act, since, without it, like the skinned Selkie, the Merrow cannot return home. In this way they may fall prey to men and become the slave of a human master, who might demand wishes or even marriage. In Italy, the *Folletti* are equally sought for their caps, which if caught by a human, bring a reward of gold.

The fairies went from the world, dear,
Because men's hearts grew cold:
And only the eyes of children see
What is hidden from the old …

KATHLEEN FOYLE

above: **Illustration from *Elfin Song*, Florence Harrison, 1912, British**

Magical transformations

Being able to change form is a powerful attribute. We have always held in awe people, such as blacksmiths, who can cause metal to become liquid and then solidify again. Also magic are substances such as glass that become fluid enough from stable form to be poured or blown. Things that are firm to the touch, but can alter are unnerving, as is being able to transcend barriers, such as skin, that keep things where we think they should be. By transforming, a fairy reveals her greatest power: to manifest in the mortal world something that is so obviously faery.

How much more impressive this is to humans than simple invisibility. Fairies use their "glamor," or powers of enchantment, to change form, for they relish metamorphosis. The Norwegian *Fossegrim*, guardian of waterfalls, can change in an instant from male to female, Russia's freshwater *Rusalka* from maid to fish to toad. Any alluring male or female in a wood or by a lake who seems more perfect than the day and by whom one is instantly smitten may be a fairy. It is through shape-shifting that the fay are able to seduce men and women, binding mortals to themselves not through love but by magic.

Some spirits come to be identified with a particular animal; others shift between forms almost randomly, from swan to goat to toad to crow. Bird forms are common: wise owl, bird of the night and of magical knowledge; powerful eagle, another bird with supernatural powers in North American, Moroccan, and Russian legend; the bird of divine fortune, the wren, who might be mistaken for a tiny winged form flitting in the undergrowth. Red deer are a common shape for Scottish Highland fairies; hunters often encounter them in this guise. A horse is an elemental magic form to many European peoples, and has the advantage of luring unsuspecting humans to climb aboard before cantering off to another world. The Swedish *Näcken* of inland waters is sometimes an old man, sometimes a boy or seductive lad, distinguishable, just, by an equine nose and flecks of green hair. But he is most powerful as a gray or white horse, tricking women and children to ride on his back, then leaping into the depths. The Scottish Kelpie inhabits moving water, particularly lochs, threatening both those who swim and those who dilly-dally by the shore. Sleek as a seal, his victims adhere to his back like glue as he leaps into the river, his body lengthening to accommodate as many children as might be playing at the water's edge.

above: **By Warwick Goble,** ***The Book of Fairy Poetry,*** **1920, British**

Shape-shifting

I'll follow you, I'll lead you
    about a round,
Through bog, through
    bush, through brake
    through brier,
Sometime a horse I'll be,
    sometime a hound,
A hog, a headless bear,
    sometime a fire;
And neigh, and bark,
    and grunt, and roar,
    and burn,
Like horse, hound, hog,
    bear, fire, at every turn.

WILLIAM SHAKESPEARE, *A MIDSUMMER*
NIGHT'S DREAM

left: **Victorian lantern slide**
The imp leads straight into the bog.

... the little old woman suddenly stood up straight, and grew tall, and young, and beautiful ...

ANDREW LANG, *THE BLUE BIRD*

right: **Suddenly a fairy appeared, Warwick Goble from *The Fairy Book,* 1923, British**
Magical transformations of old crones into dazzlingly beautiful young women are widespread in folklore and fairytale.

For just before he came to the river side, she had stept down into the cool clear water; and her shawl and her petticoat floated off her, and the green water-weeds floated round her sides, and the white water-lilies floated round her head, and the fairies of the stream came up from the bottom and bore her away and down upon their arms; for she was the Queen of them all; and perhaps of more besides.

CHARLES KINGSLEY, *THE WATER BABIES*

left: **The fairy queen, Warwick Goble from Charles Kingsley's *The Water Babies,* 1910, British**

On land, she is an an old, wrinkled woman, but in the water, the medium of transformation, she turns into a shimmering fairy.

A fairytale education

In Charles Kingsley's fairy tale *The Water Babies,* a grubby, mistreated little sweep called Tom is taken by the fairies, and enters a magical underwater world. There he is transformed into a water-baby: in the ensuing story, he not only receives a properly pious Victorian education in good behavior, but also has the most wonderful adventures. He is protected from mishaps (such as nearly being eaten by a trout) by his fairy minder, and during his travels he sees wonderful transformations: he comes across an innocent crow being set upon by the other crows because she wouldn't steal grouse eggs and other such "hoodie-crow" crimes. The fairies promptly intervened:

But the fairies took the good crow, and gave her nine new sets of feathers running, and turned her at last into the most beautiful bird of paradise with a green velvet suit and a long tail, and sent her to eat fruit in the Spice Islands, where cloves and nutmegs grow.

CHARLES KINGSLEY, *THE WATER BABIES*

right: From black crow to colorful bird of paradise, Warwick Goble from Charles Kingsley's *The Water Babies,* 1910, British

The magic box

As he nears the end of his travels, Tom is given one of the most important fairy lessons of all, in the story of Epimetheus and his wife Pandora's box of fate. He discovers hope:

"… out flew all the ills which flesh is heir to; all the children of the four great bogies, Self-will, Ignorance, Fear, and Dirt—for instance:

Measles	Famines,
Monks	Quacks,
Scarlatina	Unpaid bills,
Idols	Tight stays,
Hooping-coughs	Potatoes,
Popes	Bad Wine,
Wars	Despots,
Peacemongers	Demagogues,

And, worst of all, Naughty Boys and Girls.

But one thing remained at the bottom of the box, and that was, Hope."

CHARLES KINGSLEY, *THE WATER BABIES*

previous page: **Tom is nearly eaten by a trout, Warwick Goble from Charles Kingsley's *The Water Babies,* 1910, British**
right: **Pandora, Warwick Goble from Charles Kingsley's *The Water Babies,* 1910, British**
Tom learns that despite all the evils in Pandora's box, there is also hope.

Gifts from the fairies

… she stood there, with nothing left at all, when suddenly some stars fell down from heaven, and they were nothing else but hard shining talers, and although she had just given her shift away, she was now wearing a new one which was of the very finest linen. Then she gathered together the money into it, and was rich all the days of her life.

JACOB AND WILHELM GRIMM, *THE STAR TALERS*

left: **Illustration for *The Star Coins*, Grimm's Fairy Tales, artist unknown, 19th century, German**
The fairies gave a little girl a lifetime of wealth for her innate generosity.

Because the word 'fairy' can be traced to the Latin word *fata*, goddess of fate, she brings associations with fortune, good and bad, and also of fortunes found and lost. In return for helping fairies, mortals may be given magic gifts or worldly remuneration: silver coins left on the hob or in a shoe for a good turn done, engraved silver spoons for attending a birth, shipwrecked treasure as the dowry of a Merrow bride, wood chips in the basket that turn to gold for those who remain sensible, wise, and humble.

In fairy tales, rewards come in response to small, everyday acts of kindness: for leaving food and drink by the embers of a fire, for keeping a tidy house, or caring for a fairy child. Gifts may be also the result of bargains, or trials, for which there is also a forfeit: in return for magical transformation—of straw into gold, for example—a mortal must promise to give something up, often a first-born child. The breaking of the promise usually brings punishment.

One must be wary—and stay wary—of fairy gifts. The Leprechaun's gold coin, a bribe that distracts from his crock of gold, turns to ashes once the manikin is gone. His silver shilling is equally cunning, always returning to his purse. As for the crock of gold, the little man will disappear before you draw close to it. Gifts are more than just slippery. They have the power to overwhelm the emotions and moral code of those who use them, and have a habit of reflecting on the character of the winner. If she is virtuous, the gifts stay benevolent and the human thrives. If less than honest, breaking rules of hospitality, being selfish or bad mannered, or boasting (we are human, so this is often), bad luck draws in. In a Korean tale, a hard-working, poor couple are rewarded by seven fairies, who transport them to a magical palace to choose a gift— a purse—from which they must remove no more than one silver coin each day. But avarice and pride triumph. The husband's plans for a grand brick house necessitate more and more silver daily until the purse becomes nothing more than an old cloth bag, the unfinished brick house a tumbledown thatched cottage again.

Strange gifts challenge us to suspend our disbelief of other worlds and ways of living. In a Swiss tale, two girls taken to a fairy's baptism are rewarded with as much coal as will fill their aprons. Disgruntled with the dirty, cumbersome load, they heed not the voice shouting that the more they throw away the less they will have. After discarding much of the coal, they arrive home to find it has become pure gold. A German woman attending a birth is "smart enough" not to question, or "despise" an odd gift of shavings, which also turns to glistening gold pieces, and lives richly (curiosity is her later come-uppance).

Perhaps a fairy's most potent power derives from human fear of what might ensue if we don't obey faery rules. Rather than the showy three wishes, incantations, or magic hats, human imagination and anticipation is the essence of their power over us. Many mortals will do anything to steer clear, since fairy gold more often than not means misfortune. In giving, the fairies also take away, by playing to our human foibles, as Morgan ap Rhys discovers after winning a wish for his hospitality in an entrancing Welsh tale—an excerpt from it appears on the following pages.

Morgan ap Rhys

"Wela, wela, the wish of my heart is to have a harp that will play under my fingers. no matter how ill I strike it; a harp that will play lively tunes, look you; no melancholy music for me!" He had hardly spoken, when to his astonishment, there on the hearth before him stood a splendid harp, and he was alone. "Waw!" cried Morgan, "they're gone already." Then looking behind him he saw they had not taken the bread and cheese they had cut off; after all. "'Twas the fairies, perhaps," he muttered, but sat serenely quaffing his beer, and staring at the harp. There was a sound of footsteps behind him, and his wife came in from out doors with some friends. Morgan feeling very jolly, thought he would raise a little laughter among them by displaying his want of skill upon the harp. So he commenced to play—oh, what a mad and capering tune it was! "Waw!" said Morgan, "but this is a harp. Holo! what ails you all?" For as fast as he played his neighbors danced, every man, woman, and child of them all footing it like mad creatures. Some of them bounded up against the roof of the cottage till their heads cracked again others spun round and round, knocking over the furniture; and, as Morgan went on thoughtlessly playing, they began to pray to him to stop before they should be jolted to pieces. But Morgan found the scene too amusing to want to stop; besides, he was enamored of his own suddenly developed skill as a musician; and he twanged the strings and laughed till his sides ached and the tears rolled down his cheeks, at the antics of his friends. Tired out at last he stopped, and the dancers fell exhausted on the floor, the chairs, the tables, declaring the diawl himself was in the harp. "I know a tune worth two of that," quoth Morgan, picking up the harp again; but at sight of this motion all the company vanished from the house and escaped, leaving Morgan rolling merrily in his chair. Whenever Morgan got a little tipsy after that, he would get the harp and set everybody round him to dancing; and the consequence was he got a bad name, and no one would go near him. But all their precautions did nor prevent the neighbors from being caught now and then, when Morgan took his revenge by making them dance till their legs were broken, or some other damage was done them. Even lame people and invalids were compelled to dance whenever they heard the music of this diabolical telyn. In short, Morgan so abused his fairy gift that one night the good people came and took it away from him, and he never saw it more. The consequence was he became morose, and drank himself to death—a warning to all who accept from the fairies favors they do not deserve.

WIRT SIKES, *BRITISH GOBLINS WELSH FOLK LORE,*
FAIRY MYTHOLOGY, LEGENDS AND TRADITIONS

Fairy baby care

A fairy penchant for stealing away babies and women, particularly midwives and nursing mothers able to "lend" milk, is not Puck's mischievous leading astray for a bit of a laugh. This is stealing for a purpose, akin to the taking of grain and milk, staples to feed their community; for fairy folk need human women to attend their labors and naming ceremonies, and to suckle their young. Fairies are often humanoid in form, and they seem to require human milk to sustain them—usually in the form of a human wet nurse. Fairy formula just doesn't seem to be strong enough, or at least not for the infants of the gentry fairies.

Bright Eyes, Light Eyes! Daughter of a Fay!
I had not been a married wife a twelvemonth and a day,
I had not nursed my little one a month upon my knee,
When down among the blue bell banks rose elfins three
    times three:
They griped me by the raven hair, I could not cry for fear,
They put a hempen rope around my waist and dragged
    me here;
They made me sit and give thee suck as mortal
    mothers can,
Bright Eyes, Light Eyes! strange and weak and wan!

ROBERT WILLIAMS BUCHANAN, *THE FAIRY FOSTER MOTHER*

above: **By Warwick Goble,** *The Book of Fairy Poetry,* **1920, British**

Fetch me that flower: the herb I showed thee once.
The juice of it, on sleeping eyelids laid,
Will make or man or woman madly dote,
Upon the next live creature that it sees

WILLIAM SHAKESPEARE, *A MIDSUMMER NIGHT'S DREAM*

left: **Oberon and Titania, Warwick Goble from *The Fairy Book,*
1923, British**
While Titania is sleeping. the fairy king Oberon uses a magic herb to
confuse her perceptions as soon as she wakes up.

Fairy ointment

Fairies have always known how to use special potions to deceive the eye and confuse perception. They even use them on each other—the most famous example of this is from Shakespeare's *A Midsummer Night's Dream*. Oberon, king of the fairies, plays a trick on his fairy queen Titania by using the juice of the Love-in-Idleness flower to make her fall madly in love with the first creature she sets eyes upon when she wakes up. The ensuing chaos makes for a spell-binding, action-filled plot. And if fairies themselves fall under the spell of altered perceptions, humans are even more susceptible. A fairy can change a human being's perceptions with a mere touch.

"Where are we going, sir?" says I.
"You'll soon know," says he, and he drew his fingers across my eyes, and not a stim remained in them."
… The fingers went the other way across my eyes, and there we were before a castle door, and in we went through a big hall and great rooms all painted in fine green colors, with red and gold bands and ornaments, and the finest carpets and chairs and tables and window curtains, and fine ladies and gentlemen walking about.

PATRICK KENNEDY, *LEGENDARY FICTIONS OF THE IRISH CELTS*

When mortals are "borrowed," and see the fairy world in all its glitter and glamor, they may come in contact with a substance called fairy ointment. This is a very old story theme, with dozens of variations, dating from the thirteenth century. Often, a salve or oil is spread by the fairy onto a visitor's eyes to disguise the route. When next that person's eyes are wiped, he (or more usually she) is in fairyland. Very often the curious mortal discovers the potion's powers independently, after seeing fairy adults smear it on their own children's eyes, or after being handed it to massage into fairy neonates. By human curiosity or by accident the visitor applies a touch of ointment to one eye and is enlightened to the true nature of fairyland: the food is dung, the glorious palace a dark cave. It is now also possible to move back and forth between worlds by blinking alternate eyes.

On return to the mortal world, those who have had a touch of fairy salve retain this "fairy sight," the ability to see fairies when they mingle with mankind, especially in fairs and marketplaces, where they go to steal disguised as humans or in invisible caps or cloaks. When the fairies spy a mortal catching them out, they touch, strike, or blow the affected eye, which is left blind thereafter. In the ballad of Tam Lin, an essential source of fairy lore, the fairy queen threatens to remove the transported knight's human eyes and replace them with the eyes of a tree. Being able to see in both worlds is not a gift, but worthy of punishment.

Tomorrow I brew, today I bake,
And then the child away I'll take;
For little deems my little dame
That Rumpelstiltzkin is my name!"

WILHELM AND JACOB GRIMM, *RUMPELSTILTZKIN*

right: **Rumpelstiltzkin, Anne Anderson, from *The Briar Rose Book*, 1874–1940s, British**
Secret names and chants that must be decoded are a commonly used theme in folklore and fairytale.

Secret names

Fairy tales in which riddles and secret names are used occur frequently. In some stories fairy power holds only for as long as the mortal remains unaware of a fairy's true name. The power inherent in a magic name is immense; whoever has knowledge of the name controls the bearer of the name. It is said of trolls that they have power over human beings until their names are discovered; when a troll's name is uttered out loud, he loses his potency and his life, shattering into shards of stone. This echoes beliefs in some traditions that naming offers the person who speaks power over the named.

In some Native American communities each person takes a public name and a private name, the latter never given away, for fear of depleting life energy. In Hawaii, a name spoken out loud takes on a life of its own and influences how one develops through life. Withholding it is a positive act of protection. When the name is uttered as part of a rhyme, or magic formula, it becomes more potent, for as well as being a word-spell or mantra, it acts as an *aide-memoire* for those who overhear it. The best-known version of this is in the Grimm brothers' *Rumpelstiltzkin*, or its many equivalents, such as the English Tom Tit Tot.

Sili go Dwt

At Nant Corfan, in Cwm Tafolog, in Montgomeryshire, there once lived a poor woman who had been left a widow, with a little baby. "Whosoever hath, to him shall be given, and he shall have more abundance; but whosoever hath not, from him shall be taken away even that he hath." This was the case with the poor widow, for the Gwylliaid Cochion, the Red Banditti, of Mawddwy, sent one of their number down her chimney, although she had put scythes in it to prevent such an entry, and robbed her of all the money which she had put by to pay the rent. Not content with that, they drove away all her cattle to their lairs.

The poor woman was weeping as if her heart would break, when suddenly there came a knock at the door, and a tall old lady, dressed in green, came in with a long staff in her hand. "Why are you weeping?" asked the green lady. And the widow told her of her great misfortunes.

"Be comforted," said the stranger, "for I have gold here more than enough to pay your rent and to buy cattle to replace those which these wicked robbers have taken away." With that she brought out a great bag from under her cloak, and poured out a great heap of yellow gold on the little round table by the fire. The widow's eyes glistened and her mouth watered at the sight. "All this will I give you," said the green lady, "if you will give me what I ask for." "I will give you anything I have in my possession," said the widow: her belongings were so few that the best of them, she thought, would be a very poor exchange for the gold which was gleaming bright in the light of the peat fire. "I am not unreasonable," said the green lady, "and I always like to do a good turn for a small reward. All I ask is that little boy lying in the cradle there."

The widow felt as if she had been stabbed to the heart, and she begged and prayed the fairy (for such, it was now clear, she was) to take anything rather than take her little boy. "No," said the fairy, "you must let me have your baby. I cannot by the law we live under take him until the third day. I will come back with the gold the day after to-morrow, and if you want the gold you know the condition. But stay, if you can then tell me my right name I will not take your boy." With that she gathered up the yellow metal into her bag and went out.

The poor widow was more wretched than ever. Much as she longed for the fairy's money, she loved her little son more than all the gold on earth, and the very thought of losing him kept her from sleeping all night. The next day she went to some relatives at Llanbrynmair to see whether they could help her in her trouble, but though they had the heart they had not the means to succor her, and she had to return empty-handed. As she was going through a wood she saw an open space among the trees, and in the middle of it was a fairy ring. A little woman was dancing wildly round this ring by herself and singing. The widow could not hear the words of the song from where she was, so she crept as silently as a mouse within hearing distance. Then she heard:

"How the widow would laugh if she was aware

That *Sill go Dwt* is the name that I bear."

When the widow heard this she felt as if a ton weight had been lifted off her heart: she stole away as noiselessly as she had approached, and made for home as fast as her legs would carry her.

The next day the fairy came again, as she had said, in the guise of a tall old lady as before, dressed in green and with a long staff in her hand. She poured the gold on the little table by the fire once more, and said that. the widow could have it if she either gave up her baby or guessed her name. The widow thought that she would have some sport with the fairy, and she asked:

"How many guesses will you give me?" "As many as you like," said the fairy. Then the widow tried every strange name that she had ever heard of, all the English names she remembered, and old Welsh names like *Garmy, Gorasgwrn, Rhelemon, Enrydreg, Creiddylad, Ellylw. Gwaedan, Rathtyeu, Corth, Tybiau, Cywyllog, Peithian*. But the fairy shook her head at each. Then the widow said," I will have one more guess. Is your name *Sili go Dwt,* by any chance?" The fairy went up the chimney in a blaze of fire, such was her rage and disappointment. With the gold she left behind her the widow paid the rent and bought cattle, and there was enough to fill an old stocking besides.

W. JENKYN THOMAS, *THE WELSH FAIRY BOOK*

She has a little silver wand,
And when a good child goes to bed
She waves her wand from left to right
And makes a circle round her head.

THOMAS HOOD, *THE DREAM FAIRY*

right: **A Christmas Tree Fairy, Lizzie [Lawson] Mack, c. 1890, British**
The fairy wand focuses and directs magic power with precision.

A CHRISTMAS TREE FAIRY

Fairy wands divine

Like wings, wands are a defining part of modern fairy iconography; for instance, you just can't imagine the fairy on top of the Christmas tree without one. However, they are rarely, if ever, present in the collections of tales and lore that gave us much of our knowledge of little folk. Wands recall the power of nature that spirits such as the Wood-wives embody. The wand hewn from the fairy trees hazel, ash, rowan, or willow symbolizes nature's magical energies. As a bare stick, it resembles the dormant power of the deciduous tree in winter, which contains within it the power to bud and sprout new life when the time is right. It represents the life-force.

The tree metaphor reminds us of the deep energy of the earth that nourishes its roots, the energy of the sun and light, which ensures its greenness, and the energy of the heavens to which its branches reach. To hold a stick with thoughtful intent is to bring oneself into alignment with these forces. To wave the wand is to be as a nature spirit conducting this magic, bringing it to a point of intense focus at the tip, hence that glowing star of energy beaming out. In classical mythology the wand may be the rod of Hermes, messenger of the spirit realm. In rituals of Wicca a wand is used to describe a ritual circle, that magical, place of boundaries, of within and without, which brings us back to where we started, at the fairy ring.

Fairies are mixed up in modern minds not only with the magical wand, but with scrying, or revealing fortunes. This is not necessarily how they were thought of in the past. But this addition is important to modern fairy believers looking for benevolent supernatural helpers to validate lifestyle choices. We use fairies as allies now rather than being scared of them, adopting them as guardians to help us through times of transition by validating a career choice or lover.

Fairies have possessed powers of divination for centuries. This is most often seen in action in deciding the fate of newborn babes and helping humans divine love matches at times in the year when the door between the fairy world and our world is wedged open: St Agnes Eve, Midsummer Eve, and Hallowe'en. The mirrors and pools of still water that feature in divination customs common to these dates offer a way of looking at and looking through, and of shifting between the two, like the act of passing to a fairy world and back again. While mischievous fairies have a reputation for being unable to resist hiding objects around the home, now they are invoked as a source of knowledge to locate lost items, from jewelry to love, in the form of fairy divination cards.

The fairy beam upon you,
The stars to glister on you,
A moon of light
In the noon of night,
Till the fired rake hath o'er-gone you.
The wheel of fortune guide you,
The boy with the bow beside you
Run aye in the way
Till the bird of day
And the luckier lote betide you.

BEN JONSON

In olde days of the King Artour,
Of which the Bretons speken gret honor,
All was this lond fulfilled of faerie;
The elf-quene, with hire joly compagnie,
Danced ful oft in many a grene mede.
This was the old opinion as I rede;

GEOFFREY CHAUCER

... most in a half-circle watch'd the sun;
And a sweet sadness dwelt on everyone;
I knew not why, – but know that sadness dwells
On Mermaids – whether that they ring the knells
Of seamen whelm'd in chasms of the mid-main,
As poets sing; or that it is a pain
To know the dusk depths of the ponderous sea,
The miles profound of solid green, and be
With loath'd cold fishes, far from man – or what; –
I know the sadness but the cause know not.

chapter 7
Fairies on the Margins

When the first baby laughed for the first time, his laugh broke into a million pieces, and they all went skipping about. That was the beginning of fairies.

JAMES BARRIE, *THE LITTLE WHITE BIRD*

right: **A laugh a day ... Mabel Lucie Attwell postcard, c. 1930, British**
Fairies (and angels) are said to be drawn to the sound of laughter.

Vulnerable moments

Just as fairies congregate at the borderlands of the mortal world—on the seashore, in the forest on the edge of the village, at the crossroads, on the threshold of the home—and taboos and stories gather around these places, so too they lie in wait at mankind's emotional borders, especially the crossing places between two states of being. The daily edges when sleep falls and lifts, the turning of the seasons, life's points of flux: birth and baptism, marriage and death. And so fairy lore and protective charms tend to gather in around these experiences, too. Some commentators say fairies can't resist these liminal, or transitional, times because they require human life force with which to do their glamor; and where is that force most conspicuous? In pregnant mothers, newborn babies, and fecund couples.

Fairy tales relate how spirits such as the goblin Rumplestiltzkin were on the lookout for babies, even before they had been born. A laboring mother must be protected with red thread around her wrist or iron nails driven into the bed because this is a perilous time of transition for mother and baby, when spirits are abroad and protection and strength most required. Good fairies might be in attendance to speed the transition; or those with more mischievous intent to draw out the metamorphosis, thus prolonging danger. It is women and babies who are most at risk of abduction by fairies and so must be watched 24/7 by other mortals.

This vigilance continues after the birth until the mother rejoins the sanctified community in a churching ceremony or other form of ritual purification. Until this time she is ripe for plucking by fairy folk, especially if she undertakes journeys or sets to manual labor. All this explains why guardian spirits are valued all over the world.

- *Chang Hsien* protects Chinese mothers in childbirth, pictured as an old bearded man, occasionally accompanied by a young child.
- To the Yoruban laboring mother of Nigeria comes the Puck-like trickster *Eshu,* with his enormously complicated shaft of hair.
- The Norwegian and Danish *Huldra*, guardian spirit of the woods, gathers to her protective skirts the souls of infants who die before baptism. Since the unblessed, unnamed soul is unfinished, she takes it as her own, and can be seen trailing ghost children through the woods.

Fortune fairies arrive to tell a newborn's future, as they have since ancient Egyptian times, dictating whether this child will be happy or unfulfilled, rich or poor, when he or she will die, and how. The Albanian *Fatit* wing in mounted on butterflies on day three. In Brittany the *Béfind* is made welcome with a table of food laid out in the birthing chamber. The classical form of these fairies, ancient Greece and Rome's three Fates, are pictured with spindles, teasing out a new thread of life from the potential of a mess of wool, yet also deciding when to cut that thread.

The very word fairy derives in the Romance languages from the word "fate," in the Latin *fata*, from *fatum* or goddess of destiny. Some, like Slavic prophetic visitors, might inscribe the child's fortune in words only the fairies can read on her forehead. In many traditions the mother is actually able to see the fairy. Entwined in the notion of fate fairies are guardian spirits, who in some traditions join the watch over a baby only after baptism, when finally he or she receives a name, and so can connect with ancestor guardians.

next page: **Rumpelstilzkin arrives, Warwick Goble from *The Fairy Book*, 1923, British**
The dwarf is visiting the baby that he hopes to "win" from its mother.

Good luck befriend thee Son; for at thy birth
The Faiery Ladies daunc't upon the hearth;
Thy drowsie Nurse hath sworn she did
　　them spie
Come tripping to the Room where thou
　　didst lie;
And sweetly singing round about thy Bed
Strew all their blessings on thy
　　sleeping Head.

JOHN MILTON, *AT A VACATION EXERCISE IN THE COLLEGE*

left: **Fairies on guard, Warwick Goble, *The Book of Fairy Poetry,***
1920, British
The first days of a baby's life are the most risky—as every fairy knows.

296

Nursery spirits

As children grow older, parents invoke fairy forces to ensure they toe the line. French mothers warn of goblins hiding in the home, gobbling children up or carrying them away if they don't behave. From the Teutonic tradition comes the Sandman: the child never dares open an eye for fear of what he might do to them. Other nursery spirits are more benign: in France *La Dormette de Poitou* protects children at rest, ensuring sweet dreams. Her equivalent in Denmark is Old Close Your Eyes, Ole *Luk Øj*, the man with a silken jacket who blows fairy dust into the eyes to ensure drowsiness before opening one of two umbrellas. One is filled on the inside with beautiful images to ensure good dreams, the other, blank within, brings a dreamless sleep to naughty children.

left: The Sandman, Woldemar Friedrich, 1893, German
Just a sprinkle will send them to sleep.

The man in the moon

Young folk who can't go to sleep often gaze at the friendly face of the man in the moon, and wonder how he came to be all the way up there. Some traditions say that he was put there by the fairies!

So here in the misty moon I pine
As long as the fairy wills,
And I powder your old earth with gold,
And silver the seas and rills.

FLORENCE HARRISON, *THE MAN IN THE MOON*

right: **The Man in the Moon from *Elfin Song*, Florence Harrison, 1912, British**

A little boy wonders how that faraway face on the moon got there.

She left elf babies in their cots,
Whose eyes were like forget-me-nots,
And like the yellow grape their skin,
Their ears so pointed, long, and thin,
And hair as green as waters deep,
The mothers sing not these to sleep,
But sit and weep, and weep, and weep,
Beside the Willow River.

FLORENCE HARRISON, *THE CHANGELINGS*

left and next page: **Changelings from** *Elfin Song,* **Florence Harrison,
1912, British**

The fairies are said to steal babies and leave strange creatures in the crib. .

Changelings

From Europe comes the ubiquitous tale of why you should never leave a newborn child unguarded, even for an instant. Mothers turn back to the crib to find, not their precious infant, but an ugly, misshapen and often elderly, fairy "child"—a changeling. In some accounts it is not even alive; just a badly shaped log or block of wax. The tiny mortal has been spirited away by elves, trolls or other underground folk. Or irt might have been whisked away by that most notorious of all child abductors, Titania, queen of the fairies.

Often the fire has died out or the light been snuffed, a sign of the adults' negligence in choosing perhaps to sleep, venture outdoors for a bunch of ripe, red cherries or to gossip with neighbors instead of maintaining a constant watch. Newborns, tales state, are particularly at risk for the first three days of life (when they must be watched day and night) and to a lesser degree for the first six weeks, when they must be watched assiduously, until the safety of baptism, "there must always be a burning light near them, even in broad daylight, because the underground people are afraid of light" states nineteenth-century folklore collector J. D. H. Temme.

Interestingly, current neonatal practice approves these measures: newborn babies must be kept warm, in light, and in our presence not for fear of underground folk, but to ward off jaundice, SIDS, and because before four weeks infants cannot conserve warmth.

She never had so sweet a changeling;
And jealous Oberon would have the child
Knight of his train, to trace the forests wild;
But she perforce withholds the loved boy,
Crowns him with flowers and makes him
    all her joy:

WILLIAM SHAKESPEARE, *A MIDSUMMER NIGHT'S DREAM*

Fairies prefer boy babies

Male babies are most prized by fairy folk, the unbaptised most at risk. In some tales we hear how the human child has been chosen for good looks, to bring earthly beauty to the gene pool of the underground race. In other tales children are taken for slaves, to serve or amuse the fay. Very occasionally we follow the child to the fairy hill in which he or she is kept captive, sometimes with treatment mirroring the actions of human parents to the strange "infant" above. Shakespeare, in *A Midsummer Night's Dream,* dramatizes the fate of "A lovely boy, stol'n from an Indian King" and whisked to the fairy court, where he is crowned with flowers as Titania makes him "all her joy" in a lover's battle of will and desire with her own husband-king, Oberon. Many such children, tales tell, pine away from lack of mortal food, but others are entranced by their new world, only withering away when restored to their human home. In Japanese tales if the human child eats or drinks in fairyland before the parents discover the identity theft, he or she can never go home.

left: **Titania and her changeling, Arthur Rackham, from *Shakespeare's A Midsummer Night's Dream,* first published 1908, British**
The fairy queen had plotted to steal the exotic baby of an Indian king.
next page: **Titania and Puck, unfinished picture by George Romney, engraved by Edward Scriven, c. 1815**
Titania is openly exultant about her theft of a baby boy.

Desperate parents

Back in the parents' home, the changeling, or *killcrop* in the German tradition, lies sickly and wizened, commonly with shrunken legs and an abnormally large head, either never gaining the power of speech, or displaying frighteningly precocious language skills. It howls incessantly and feeds ravenously, suckling so greedily, says one tale, that it empties the mother and five wet nurses, but is still not sated. A Scottish story describes how a changeling "bit and tore its mother's breasts" so insatiable was its hunger. In bleeding the home of food and drink and howling inhumanly day and night, it threatens the very existence of the family. Moreover, these "children" never grow up; in some tales they are thought to be generations old, always as ravenous and overwhelming to care for as a newborn. In some cases, the selfless devotion of the parents to this difficult child, despite their mourning, results in the return of the beloved birth child.

In many changeling tales, the stricken parents seek advice from a neighbor, wise woman, curate, or landlord, who urges a course of action. Most often, the advice is that the "beastly child" will give away its true identity by expressing surprise, or laughing on encountering something strange. Commonly, the parents are urged to place the child on the kitchen floor, kindle a fire, and begin to cook a harvest supper, or brew beer in an egg or walnut shell. Astounded, the "child" cries out, revealing a disproportionate size, strength, or power of speech—and its true age and status. It might be a dwarf husband with many sons of his own, or a useless, aged fairy, dumped by the tribe for younger blood. Once unmasked, the changeling disappears and the true child may return, sometimes smuggled in by fairy folk.

Much crueler accounts describe the testing of a "changed" child, one who once so lusty in health and good nature, suddenly becomes ugly, loses his senses and speech, and acts as wild as an animal. In some tales the changeling is tossed onto hot coals or put to bake in the oven, with the loaves. In other tales community or religious figures urge parents to throw the creature into a river, abandon it on a cold hillside or atop a dung pile, salt him, or beat it with birch switches. Sadly, Northern European court records from the seventeenth and nineteenth centuries show that such tortures were inflicted on real children who did not fit in. The German religious leader, Martin Luther, decreed that a changeling, or "malformed" child, was the work of Satan, and deserved only abuse and destruction.

Consequently, a covert defense for child beatings, neglect, even infanticide, was that the child was a changeling. Oscar Wilde's father, Sir William Wilde, denounced cruel "exorcisms" conducted in Ireland against suspected changeling children as late as 1854. His mother, Lady Wilde, wrote in 1887 that, "This superstition makes the peasant-women often very cruel towards weakly children." Compare these accounts with contemporary news reports of the exorcisms of African children accused of *ndoki*, possession by evil spirits. Far from being a fanciful fairy tale, the notion of a changeling reflects themes that disturb modern parents now as ever: the fear that an infant will fail to thrive, or have mental or behavioral disorders; the horror of parental neglect; the panic when a child goes missing.

next page: **Riddling a changeling, J Copland, in *J. Maxwell Wood's Witchcraft in south-western Scotland,* 19th Century, British**
Holding a changeling over rowan smoke was said to break the fairy spell.

The Changeling

Every intelligent grandmother knows that the fire must not be allowed to go out in a room where there is a child not yet christened; that the water in which the newborn child is washed should not be thrown out; also, that a needle, or some other article of steel must be attached to its bandages. If attention is not paid to these precautions it may happen that the child will be exchanged by the trolls, as once occurred in Bettna many years ago.

A young peasant's wife had given birth to her first child. Her mother, who lived some distance away, was on hand to officiate in the first duties attending its coming, but the evening before the day on which the child should be christened she was obliged to go home for a short time to attend to the wants of her own family, and during her absence the fire was allowed to go out.

No one would have noticed anything unusual, perhaps, if the child had not, during the baptism, cried like a fiend. After some weeks, however, the parents began to observe a change. It became ugly, cried continuously, and was so greedy that it devoured everything that came in its way. The people being poor, they were in great danger of being eaten out of house and home. There could no longer be any doubt that the child was a changeling. Whereupon the husband sought a wise old woman, who, it was said, could instruct the parents what to do to get back their own child.

The mother was directed to build a fire in the bake oven three Thursday evenings in succession, lay the young one upon the bake shovel, then pretend that she was about to throw it into the fire. The advice was followed, and when the woman, the third evening, was in the act of throwing the changeling into the fire, it seemed, a little deformed, evil-eyed woman rushed up with the natural child, threw it in the crib, and requested the return of her child. "For," said she, "I have never treated your child so badly and I have never thought to do it such harm as you now propose doing mine," whereupon she took the unnatural child and vanished through the door.

HERMAN HOFBERG, FROM *SWEDISH FAIRY TALES*, TRANSLATED BY W. H. MYERS

Protective charms for babies

Amulets for the cradle were considered so important in some regions of the world that the plain wooden box was festooned, and must have looked quite as frou-frou as some modern Moses baskets. The child hidden within should be watched day and night, maybe for a whole year lest spirits had their evil way. Jacob Grimm suggested that neglectful mothers who fell asleep at night should not be surprised if their children were substituted.

Tied threads A red thread tied around wrist, neck, or ankle across Europe and Central Asia (in parts of Africa it is a white thread or beads) has protective powers when it sits next to the skin, at pulse points where you can see the life force (red is symbolic of blood, the stuff that keeps us in this world). Mothers might even mark bed linen with a stitch of red. In Italy it becomes a talismanic red coral pendant or teether; in Thailand a tiny silver bracelet hung with a bell and clasped around the ankle, its circle a powerful symbol of protection, since it is complete, with no hole permitting entry. Ornate braided knots fasten baby clothes in Japan and China, and golden knots might be given in Japan as a baby gift.

Cross-dressing Dressing boys as girl babies was thought in Albania, as in other cultures, to confuse the *Djinn*. Hats placed on Chinese babies disorientate bad spirits, who see in the cradle a flower (girl) or a tiger (boy), not a baby. Earflaps on the hat protect another potential point of entry. In Rajasthan babies' eyes are lined with black kohl, black being an amuletic color. The custom of dressing boys in blue may derive from the protective nature of this color, which deflects the evil eye.

Pins and needles A needle threaded with red silk on the nursing mother's shirt protects a baby by safeguarding his milk supply, the deterrent sharpness of the point as important as the lucky color. Thus, the safety pin in a cloth diaper protects on two levels. The points of a triangle are similarly effective, carrying also the luck of the trinity. In Central Asia, triangles are embroidered or woven into curtains, cushions and hangings, some pierced with a needle. In Turkmenistan a broken needle forms part of the adornment of a baby's cap. In North Cornwall mothers were advised to pin their children to their clothing to prevent them from being stolen away. In parts of Africa, piercing the ears of month-old infants guards another site of entry, the ear, from ingress.

Knives and scissors In Eastern Europe, knives and scissors might hang from baby amulets, or even be placed in the cradle. Any sharp steel implement was thought effective when placed in the cradle, thought Danish mothers, a habit they took to America. Welsh women advised laying a pair of fire tongs across the cradle.

Bells The tinkling of bells keeps spirits airborne, preventing them from alighting, and so they hang from amulets and wind chimes, and are placed in rattles and toys. In Christian counties they recall church bells. Any metallic jingle will serve, metal being powerfully effective against evil: the tinkle and crash of buttons and beads, coins and cowry shells is heard all over the world, but especially across Asia. They are sewn to baby's hats, hems, seams and closings—gaps an opportunistic spirit might slip through.

Eye motifs A shiny eye, like mirrors and glittery trinkets, attracts the evil eye, and reflects back its evil intentions, repelling the evil-doer. The power of like cures like is especially invoked across the Islamic world and the Mediterranean by blue glass beads, from a single bead on a thong around a child's neck to elaborate stylized eyes adorning a Turkish amulet pinned to a child's dress or hung near the cradle.

The word of God The Bible, a hymnbook, or a page thereof might be placed in the cradle or near a child's head. Hindus might slip a sutra, Muslims verses from the *Qur'an* into a silver amulet case worn around the neck.

left: **A well-protected baby, Illustration by L.M. in *Pretty Polly*, c. 1890 British**
The metal bells used in rattles and baby toys are traditionally believed to frighten away malevolent spirits.

When one of Lisa's baby teeth fell out here, the tooth fairy left her 50 cents. Another tooth fell out when she was with her father in Las Vegas, and that tooth fairy left her $5. When I told Elvis that 50 cents would be more in line, he laughed. He knew I was not criticizing him; how would Elvis Presley know the going rate for a tooth?

PRISCILLA PRESLEY

right: **Fairy from *Elfin Song*, Florence Harrison, 1912, British**

The tooth fairy

We may not all believe in fortune fairies, but the tooth fairy is ubiquitous, celebrated in books, collecting banks, and pillows, and at the dentist's office, prettifying promotional literature. She is a protective and fortune fairy, preventing detached milk teeth from being used for magic purpose, and leaving a token of her appreciation. She appears while children are sleeping to retrieve the fallen tooth hidden beneath the pillow. If she rewards with a coin, it should be silver (metal governed by the moon). In France she might bring a small toy, in Slovenia, tooth-rotting candy. The fairy also shape-shifts: in Spanish-speaking countries she is the tooth mouse.

With the loss of milk teeth begins another transition stage, from preschool child based at home with family and familiar carers, to the school child away from home for many hours, just big enough to look after himself without mommy. Since the tooth fairy attends the child from age five to age eight or even nine, she accompanies him through this period of change, to the point at which he no longer needs to believe. The tooth fairy comes alive again when the child becomes a parent himself. To those who have spent years in the cut-and-thrust adult world where fairies are few and far between, this reclaiming of a warm home life and ancestral lore can be very special.

Although the tooth fairy is a twentieth-century spirit, rituals surrounding first teeth have existed since ancient times. Viking mythology tells that the gods gave a tooth-gift to Freyja and it seems that mortals followed the custom, offering children something to mark the first tooth emerging through the gum, and the coming of weaning, a transitional time of breaking away from total reliance on the mother.

Teeth are powerful signs of identity that survive death, decay, and burial. This disturbed many cultures, since malign spirits were thought to be able to be empowered by the DNA contained within, and forever hold sway over the person the tooth described. The possessions of children are charged with life energy, making them much coveted by the spirit world. Since teeth form within the womb, they also recall life before birth, often seen as a realm of spirits or fairies. Teeth therefore are routinely burned, reabsorbed by the parent by swallowing (by the household puppy in Mongolia), or buried, connoting notions of regrowth. In other parts of the world, including Austria, the tooth is made into a piece of protective jewelry. In Japan, a top tooth would be thrown to the heavens, lobbed over the roof of the home, the bottom tooth cast beneath the floor, a piece of sympathetic magic to encourage strong growth upward and downward.

The enchanting bride

Because of the possibility of fairy spirits lifting away a bride, particularly just before or during a ceremony, when she is at her most beautiful and sexually alluring, she is protected with a veil, dummy brides (bridesmaids and matrons of honor), the supportive arm of a senior male from her close family, and all sorts of propitiating and protective measures, ranging from items of blue, sprigs of rosemary and amuletic flowers, to silver in the shoe and henna-painted hands and feet. In many cultures family and friends play variations of games based on a "hunt the bride" theme.

Bridegrooms don't get off lightly either. There are many tales that tell of a groom being lured from his mortal wife-to-be by an unearthly belle just before the wedding. The wedding night is another time when spirits await the much-anticipated consummation; the traditional thing to do is throw a surprise shivaree. Friends and family hide outside (or even within) the wedding chamber, pots and pans at the ready to give up a great clanging that rids the space of love-lorn fairies and merits the reward of fine food and drink.

left: **Young bride, artist unknown, from *Allers Familj Journal*, 1925, Swedish**
A new bride may be spirited away at this vulnerable time of transition, so she is traditonally veiled, guarded with attendants and carries a variety of charms and amulets to ward off danger.

Funeral fairies

They are clearly seen by those men of the Second Sight to eat at funerals and banquets; hence many will not taste meat at these meetings lest they have communion with, or be poisoned by them.

ROBERT KIRK, *THE SECRET COMMONWEALTH OF ELVES, FAUNES AND FAIRIES*

Some fairies only make themselves known immediately before the moment of death. The Icelandic *Fylgja* is such a spirit, for though she is a guardian fairy who attaches to a single soul for life, she can only be seen in dreams until death approaches. The moment you see her is the moment you know the nature of your ending. The Grim is an English fairy, who wails, like the Irish Banshee, at the death of a sick person, often at a window or in the form of an owl or black dog. These are sympathetic spirits who seem genuinely disturbed by pain and death. Robert Kirk describes a more unsettling habit of the little people: their attendance at mortal funerals. The poet William Blake spoke of witnessing a more peaceful ending: a fairy funeral, "a procession of creatures of the size and color of green and gray grasshoppers, bearing a body laid out on a rose-leaf, which they buried with songs, and then disappeared."

right: **The Valkyre's Vigil, Edward Robert Hughes RWS, 1906, British**
The nordic valkyre attends and guides the dead soul to the next world.

I have gone out and seen the lands of Faery,
And have found sorrow and peace and beauty there,
And have not known one from the other, but found each
Lovely and gracious alike, delicate and fair.

. . .

I have come back from the hidden, silent lands of Faery
And have forgotten the music of its ancient streams:
And now flame and wind and the long, grey, wandering wave
And beauty and peace and sorrow are dreams within dreams.

FIONA MACLOED

Children born of fairy stock
Never need for shirt or frock,
Never want for food or fire,
Always get their hearts desire:
Jingle pockets full of gold,
Marry when they're seven years old.
Every fairy child may keep
Two ponies and ten sheep;
All have houses, each his own,
Built of brick or granite stone;
They live on cherries, they run wild –
I'd love to be a Fairy's child.

ROBERT GRAVES

chapter 8

Fairy Trees and Plants

If treated well, the fairies will discover the hidden pot of gold, and reveal the mysteries of herbs

LADY WILDE ANCIENT LEGENDS, *MYSTIC CHARMS, AND SUPERSTITIONS OF IRELAND*

Previous page: **Fairies at play among the leaves, Richard Doyle from *In Fairyland,* 1875, British**
right: **Fairy folk by an old gnarled tree, Arthur Rackham, from *Imagina,* 1914, British**
The fairies hold legendary knowledge of the magical, protective, and curative properties of trees and plants.

Fairy trees

The tree of eternity
whose roots rise on high
and whose branches reach down to earth
is pure spirit
who in truth is called non-death.
All the worlds rest in it
and beyond it no one can go.

FROM *THE KATHA UPANISHAD*

"Touch wood" is the traditional phrase to ward off assault by unwelcome forces. Trees connect us directly with the spirit realm; in many cultures they are ladders or tools of contemplation by which the human spirit ascends to commune with higher states. They make tangible in the mortal world something of the immortal realm, for, like fairies, they inhabit many spheres simultaneously: their roots in the earth, or underworld, trunk in human space, branches reaching to the heavens. And as they die each fall to be reborn in spring, they seem to hold powers of renewal and regeneration, even eternal youth and life. When the tree is no more, it stays powerful: the ashes, sanctified by fire, can be magically protective, when smeared on body, house, or animal pens. And trees, like fairies, stand for the mysteries of life and the imagination, while as symbols they help us grasp at the unknowable.

Buddha found enlightenment sitting beneath a tree; Hindus were urged to retreat into the forest as death approached to fuse with the natural world, and so find rebirth. Celtic belief says that we fuse with the essence of trees even as we act, each fingertip associated with the nature of a single tree, many of them fairy trees. The oak, ash, and thorn in particular are considered sacred to wee folk. Where these trees thrive together, fairies will be found, says northern European tradition.

But trees and their spirits are vulnerable and in need of human protection. A German Wood-wife dies each time a mortal bends a sapling or damages the bark of a single branch. Irish *Skeaghshee*, or tree spirits, who inhabit solitary trees, known as fairy trees, require farmers and road-builders to champion them if they are to survive. In Melbourne, Australia, it is children who have fought to defend a fairy tree in a city center park. The park rangers fear that decades of posted fairy letters and tiny gifts have contributed to its decay.

Hazel magic

move along these shades
In gentleness of heart; with gentle hand
Touch – for there is a spirit in the woods.

WILLIAM WORDSWORTH *NUTTING*

The hazel carries the fortune of fairy wisdom, or higher knowledge and, in Ireland, bardic ability and powers of prediction. This makes the hazel twig good material for wands and divining forks. In versions of the Cinderella story, a hazel stands in for the fairy godmother. The nuts are seen as supernatural wisdom concentrated and sealed in a shell, and are key to Hallowe'en fortune and love-divination rituals. The hazel is associated with fertility, and nut thickets are guarded by the spirit Melch Dick.

To invoke its powers
- Wrap a hazelnut in a scrap of red silk and carry in a pocket for fortune.
- Twist two hazel twigs into a cross, bind with red ribbon, then drip over the wax from a Candlemas candle, and place prominently in the home.
- For love divination, place two hazelnuts on the embers of a fire, named after lovers. If both burn, you have a strong, steady love. If one pops and flies the match is not good.

right: Hazel tree, an unattributed chromolithograph, c. 1890
Use the fairy power of hazel twigs to try your hand at water divining.

Fairy thorn

Hawthorn bloom and elder flowers
Will fill a house with evil powers

TRADITIONAL ENGLISH RHYME

The hawthorn or May Tree is bound up in the fairies' biggest annual celebration, May Day. It gains its nickname Fairy Thorn because the fairies flock beneath the boughs for meetings, some of them romantic. The tree is used also to mark out human boundaries and meeting places, and there are taboos about cutting or bringing it indoors. The blackthorn is also sacred and is guarded by the *Lunantishee* fairies. In 1999 in County Clare, Ireland, another fairy thorn, a whitethorn bush, hit the headlines. Storyteller Eddie Lenihan protested at its proposed uprooting to make way for a new road, claiming it to be a *sceach*, or fairy tree, and generations old. The road was re-routed.

Invoking its forces
- Never break a twig, nor pluck a leaf: you risk displeasing the fairies. And remember that, among Italians and Catholics, the hawthorn is regarded as the Virgin Mary's plant.
- Do not bring the blossom indoors, for fear of disaster and death.

left: **Illustration by Arthur Rackham, *Grimm's Fairy Tales,* 1909, British**
The hawthorn performs its protective role by ensnaring a witch.

Rowan charms

This red-berried tree is planted near homes for its supreme protective powers over fairy forces at home and in the dairy. Taboos against cutting it down are still heeded. Its powers are invoked at times when the fairy world is near ours, especially on the eve of May Day, when boughs might be cut, peeled, and twisted in protective circles to see off fairy thieving parties. Rowan wood is a wand and divining material, and swatches are used by fairy horsemen as whips.

Invoking its forces

- Bend a circlet from branches in the green to protect milk pails and butter churns, as in Ireland.
- Tie a twig to a cow's tail to prevent tiny folk stealing milk.
- Use a twig for stirring cream, to prevent fairy curdling.
- Burn the wood to give off protective smoke.
- Lay a baby to sleep in a cradle carved from rowan wood.
- Make a cross from twigs, splitting one to push the other through and binding with red twine or native-breed sheep's wool. On May Eve or May morning hang on barn doors and above the front door of the house (on the inside).
- Place a bundle of twigs over the bed and over internal doors.

right: Costume Design for the Fairy Mountain-Ash, from *Sleeping Beauty,* artist unknown
The strong, bright, red color of the rowan tree's berries are a major factor in its protective force.

Bakst
1921

The sacred ash

This is the cosmic tree of life, known as Yggdrasil, in Scandinavian mythology, and so well entwined with lore of little races and other worlds. Stand in the shadow of its canopy for protection from little people and never harm a branch or root. In the Celtic tree alphabet, ash is linked with the day of creation, and its healing qualities are celebrated: ash sap was even considered a tonic for newborns in Scotland. The twigs make good wands, and the leaves are useful in love divination.

Invoking its forces

- Salute the tree, or wish it good day as you pass it, raising your middle finger: Celtic lore says that the fingertip is ruled by this tree.
- Place ash berries near a cradle.
- Look for a lucky leaf—one which has even-numbered leaflets—on Midsummer Eve.

left: Yggdrasil, engraving, artist and source unknown, c. 19th century
This is the mysterious, sacred ash whose branches overhang the universe; it is the great Tree of Life, the center of Norse mythology.

Birch – the lady of the woods

Birch twigs are bound together to make excellent brooms—which, with a touch of magic, also make popular transport vehicles for fairies and witches. In Scotland the *Ghillie Dhu* inhabits the birch, tree of mysteries and secrets, according to fourteenth-century Welsh poet Gruffydd ap Dafydd. The fairies sit impishly camouflaged among its leaves and lichen, waiting to entrap travelers and whisk them for frolics in fairyland by binding them with fronds. The spirit of the birch tree in another guise is Lady of the Woods, who drifts by night and is equally feared and adored. She stands for spring and young women, but those she lays her hands on are marked, and death comes to those she touches on the heart. In Russia the tree has powers over evil spirits, who might be "birched" with a swatch of leafy twigs. Birch twigs used to whisk the skin in the banya bathhouse might also keep at bay the *Bannik* fairy that lurks beneath the stove, ready to throw hot rocks and boiling water at those who displease him.

Invoking its forces

- Plant near the home for protection.
- Carry a piece of birch bark into the home, as in Russia.

right: **Flying on broomsticks, Florence Anderson, from Lady Margaret Sackville's *The Traveling Companions,* 1915, British**
The witch and her companions use magic birch brooms for transport.

Oak and dryads

Turn your clokes
For fairy folks
Are in old oakes.

BRITISH CHARM

The more craggy, twisted, and hollow an ancient oak, the more it is likely a fairy dwells within. Squeeze through an opening between two oak trees and you will pass into fairyland, where fairies smoke acorns in their pipes. The mighty oak's magical powers were co-opted by the Christian church in leaf-carving decoration and blessings at Rogation tide in May. It is the tree of classical dryads, and in Russia, rags and ribbons are hung on its branches for *Rusalka*, the female river spirit who summers in the woods.

An oak tree is considered especially magical if mistletoe grows within its boughs—a rare occurrence. This most mystical plant seems, like fairies, to thrive between two worlds, purely, it seems to the onlooker, on light and air. This traditional protective Yule-tide evergreen has also been used in fairy magic at the other end of the year, on Midsummer Eve.

Invoking the forces
- Bind leafy swatches into a wreath to hang near the threshold.
- Oak-leaf amulets are especially effective for homes with new babies.

left: Philomen and Baucis, Arthur Rackham, from Nathaniel Hawthorne's *Wonder Book*, 1922, British
The loving old couple turn into an entwined oak and linden at their deaths.

Elder – the fairy tree

**Old girl, give me of thy wood
And I will give thee some of mine
When I grow into a tree**

BLESSING ON FELLING AN ELDER

Also known as Fairy Tree, this is another venerated shrub protective to fairies and humans alike. Planted by the back door it guards the home from evil, and an elder walking stick protects lone travelers after dark. In Scandinavian and Teutonic lore it is home to *Hylde-Moer* (Elder Mother) and so demands respect. If you pick the flowers or berries, first ask permission. Touted as nature's medicine chest, this is the most widely used plant in folk healing in Britain.

Invoking its forces

- Never burn the wood: if you do you will rouse evil spirits.
- Not good cradle material: leaves the baby open to fairy mischief.
- Try a glass of home-brewed elderberry wine to view hidden folk.
- Do not fall asleep under it: you will fall into an endless coma.
- Never bring the blossom indoors. Pick branches on May Eve and hang above doors and windows to keep out spirits.
- Make a dye and use it to stain doorstep and hearthstone.

right: **The Elder Mother, Arthur Rackham, Hans Andersen's *Fairy Tales,* 1932, British**
The fairies revere the elder for its sacred healing powers.

346

Immortal pine

In Asia, this tree represents immortality, and is planted around Chinese graves. From its resin sprout legendary mushrooms on which the immortal race of the Daoist feast. The Pueblo and Hopi Indians see it as a tree that ancestors ascended to our world of light and sun; and to many Native American peoples she is simply "grandmother," constantly green and so eternally alive and proof that all is well in spirit and human worlds. In Sweden, the pine is inhabited by Pine Tree Mary, *Tallemaja,* who is closely aligned to the predatory seductress, the *Skogsrå*. Christmas tree dressing as we know it today, with fairy atop, originated with the Norway spruce.

Who leaves the pine-tree, leaves his friend, unnerves his strength, invites his end.

RALPH WALDO EMERSON, *WOODNOTES*

left Fir tree, Arthur Rackham, Aesop's *Fables* 1912, British
Soaring toward the heavens, pine trees point the way to infinity and eternity—but their very tallness invites mortals to cut them down.

Willow and alder

These trees grow near water and thus have special powers. The willow is the Tibetan tree of life and a Daoist symbol of immortality—aptly, since it is one of first branches to bud in spring. The associations with magical rebirth and spiritual healing (Native Americans use its branches to construct sweat lodges) tally well with its very real pharmaceutical powers: the white willow has given us salicylic acid (forerunner of aspirin), effective in reducing fever, pain, and inflammation.

All this energy is channeled through willow wands. In northern Europe the willow is sacred to the moon goddess and the spirit of the tree is reputed to wander during fairy hours, following lone travelers, whispering and sighing. In a Japanese tale a man marries a willow wife, the spirit of a tree dearer to him than anything on earth, and they have a child. She dies when villagers fell the tree to construct a temple.

Guarded by water spirits, alder is another fabled riverside and wetland tree which must not be cut down. It is also known to grow over saints' wells. In Greek mythology this was a tree of resurrection because of its water-resistance. The alder may neutralize the glamor of fairies bent on malevolent ways. Its forces are strongest on Saturdays, according to Celtic lore, and are directed with the tip of the ring finger.

right: Beneath the willow tree, Ernst Dryden, 1926, Austrian
The term "willowy" denotes an elegant grace and beauty—one of the many delightful attributes of this fairy-favored tree.

Tree-dressing

A tradition much in revival, at May and midsummer as well as midwinter, tying ribbons and flags, wishes and prayers, baked and iced decorations to the branches of a tree honors the spirit, or fairy, that guards or resides within it. Red ribbons are traditional, and rags hope to effect cures for ailments associated with the part of the body from which the garment is torn. Tokens made of fabric offer up human endeavor and hard work.

German winter tree ornaments date from the 1600s: they included paper roses and gilded walnuts, apples and gingerbread, tinsel etched from silver. Toward the end of nineteenth century glass baubles came to be hung on the tree, first again in Germany. Some say the blowing of glass into baubles updated the tradition of the hollow glass witch (or watch) balls, placed since the eighteenth century in cottage windows to protect a home. Imported baubles went on sale in the Woolworth 5-cent store in 1880, and within a decade were flying out in huge volumes.

The proper adornment for the Christmas tree is not the Christian star or angel, nor the Danish paper flag, but a fairy. She represents the spirit of light triumphing at this, the darkest time of year in the northern hemisphere. And she safeguards the tree in its alien, indoor setting. She is most affecting when homemade by children: a small doll wearing a white dress, aluminum foil wings that need mending each year, and a gold paper crown. She must be placed at the apex of the tree last, before her namesake fairy lights are illuminated.

left: A dressed tree, from *Le Folklore Belge,* 1950, artist unknown
In Campine, Belgium, a *Chapelle de Mai is* hung in a May tree.

Fairy herbs

In some territories, the skill of healing with herbs is donated by fairies to those who do them good, especially by looking after fairy babies. In Russia, it is the Rusalka who offers the knowledge. Some healers attribute their expertise to inter-breeding with fairy folk generations ago. Knowledge not only of which plants to use is given by the fay, but of when to pick them. Some gain in potency by being gathered at noon or midnight, while dew-covered at May dawn, or on St. John's Eve near the midsummer solstice. Make the right selection of petals or roots and the gifts of the fairies sit well upon you. Break a branch from the wrong tree or use a herb incorrectly and you may be struck down.

Rue Makes British and Persian fairies alike powerless; grasp two handfuls to escape their world, or wear the dried leaves in a little bag around the neck. Indoors, rub the floor with this herb to set any spirits flying. Rue is used medicinally to strengthen the eyesight, though no reports state whether it brings fairy worlds into focus.

Wormwood Plant of the shade, this is one of the most important herbs in fairy ointments, used to put enchantment onto a person, or to remove it. Consume too much of its brain-stimulant constituent *thujone*, and the world turns blue, then yellow, they say. It is an ingredient of *la fée verte,* absinthe, famed for its narcotic-like effects. The herb is known to repel evil.

right: **Herb Rue, Walter Crane, from *Flowers from Shakespeare's Garden,* 1906, British**
Fairies are said to fear this herb and will fly away as soon as they see it.

Its repelling property is most popularly expressed in its folk use as a worm and flee tonic. Carry a sprig in your pocket at night to ensure safe passage through a dark wood, especially in Russia, where it is supremely effective against the Rusalka.

Wild thyme Gather from the side of a fairy hill and wear a sprig or use the tops in a potion that enables you to watch the fairy world, especially if you sleep out. When placed under the pillow, it keeps away the night mare (might this be related to its use as a respiratory tonic and to relieve muscle spasms)? Medicinally, it is valued for anti-ageing properties.

Wood sorrel Used in fairy and elf spells, maybe because of its triple-leafed habit. In the nineteenth century this plant's magical properties were co-opted to the Christian Trinity, though it retains the nickname Fairy Bells.

Yarrow A protective plant against fairy glamor, and a potent wound healer and speeder of recovery. It cannot be harmed by supernatural forces (it flowers, miraculously, until midwinter). Good to hang over the cradle. Gives powers of prediction and is used in love divination. Harvest at noon on a sunny day near full moon for concentrated potency.

Stitchwort Picking this may cause you to be pixie-led warn people in Devon, England, since it is a plant considered special by the fairies.

Elecampane The aromatic root is the active part used in fairy magic: other names for this include elf dock and elf wort. Grow or scatter around the home if you fancy drawing the little folk in. Elves also have a fondness for lavender, or elf leaf.

Ground ivy Lady Wilde tells us that ground ivy safeguards against spirits and is a cure for many fairy ills.

Clover This plant, also known as shamrock or Tom Thumbs, gains some of its supernatural powers (in weather prediction and fairy lore) from the trefoil shape of its leaves: three is a magic number. Pliny considered it sacred. Find a four-leaf clover (even better a five-leaf), make a wish, place it in your hat or behind an ear, and you will see fairies. Similarly if you concoct an ointment of four-leaf clover, or an amulet containing a clover and seven grains of wheat. Clasp a clover also to extinguish fairy glamor. Be wary about flaunting this herb: odd-leafed clovers have most potency when stumbled across rather than actively sought out, and those who carry a clover are considered fair game for fairy enchantment.

Mugwort A charm plant, placed in the shoes during journeys and famously worn proudly in the Isle of Man, scene of much fairy lore, on the national day, July 4. Mermaids like this plant. Occasionally used in a similar way to wormwood.

St. John's Wort This is the chief protective herb, healer of all ills caused by fairies, states Katharine Briggs. The flowers of this "sun herb," which blooms around the summer solstice, were burned as part of protective fire festivities associated with Midsummer Day (which coincides with St. John's Day). It acts as a charm against malicious fairies and a cure for fairy darts, since it is one of the few herbs that cannot be acted upon by supernatural forces. It may be used by Irish and Manx fairies as a steed (another name is Fairy's Horse). Carry a sprig, but don't step on it, for fear of angering the fairies.

I know a bank whereon the wild thyme blows,
Where oxlips and the nodding violet grows,
Quite over-canopied with lush woodbine,
With sweet musk-roses and with eglantine.
There sleeps Titania sometime of the night
Lull'd in these flowers with dances and delight.

WLLIAM SHAKESPEARE, *A MIDSUMMER NIGHT'S DREAM*

left: **Titania and Oberon, Walter Paget, from *Shakespeare Pictures*, date unknown, British**
Oberon, like all fairies, knows all the uses of plants, and squeezes the juice of a flower onto Titania's eyelids to alter her perceptions.

Fairy flowers

Some fairies are thought to live in the bells of flowers, such as tiny English Pilliwiggins, or rest their babies in streaked tulip blooms. Others act as guardians of certain species, or gather them for spellmaking, making some fairy flowers taboo for arrangement in the home. Shakespeare passed on much lore about fairy flowers in *A Midsummer Night's Dream,* where Oberon tells which combinations lull to sleep, and how the juice of a pansy anointed on the eye lids of someone who sleeps:

> "Will make a man or woman madly dote
> Upon the next live creature that it sees."

Primrose Fairies do not gladly pass this token of spring, wary of some flowers that are yellow in color and because it has the power to make those who are invisible visible (though in Wales and Ireland it confers invisibility). Eat a primrose and you will be able to see fairyland and all its activities; other tales say touching a certain rock with an appropriate number of blooms opens a doorway to fairyland.

Invoking its forces
- Scatter petals over the threshold and bring a posy inside, especially at May Day say some tales: never bring indoors say many others.
- Do not hang a posy on the front door if you want to avoid fairies.
- Tie a posy to cows' tails.

right: **Primrose, Walter Crane, from *Flowers from Shakespeare's Garden,* 1906, British**
The primrose reputedly gives humans the abilty to see fairies.

Daisy Make a daisy chain and place around a child's neck to protect him or her from fairy enchantment, maybe because the flowers resemble the sun with their golden brilliance and mass of pink-tinged rays. They open their faces when the sun rises, and close them at nightfall, protecting the interior from fairy ingress. In England, daisies were used in well-dressing to honor spirits of a spring, and widely applied in love divination: count "he loves me, he loves me not" with the petals, or sleep with the root beneath your pillow to bring back an errant lover.

Bluebell Bluebell woods are places of fairy enchantment and should be ventured into with awe and respect. They are places where one might be pixie-led, and children are particularly at risk. Be wary of becoming lost in enchantment here, or of hearing a bluebell ring—said to indicate certain death or the presence of a malicious spirit. Other tales say it benignly calls fairies to dance, as, in Wales, do the white bells of the wood sorrel.

Foxglove These harbingers of summer are renowned as fairy gloves, hats, thimbles, and gowns or petticoats (other names include Folk's or Fairy Gloves, Fairy Bells, Fairy Fingers, Fairy Cap, Fairy Petticoats). They may draw some of their power from association with that sly nocturnal trickster, the fox. Cultivating foxgloves or bringing them into the home attracts fairy folk, which may be why there is a taboo about picking and arranging the spires of blooms. The plant's sap has the power to break fairy spells (beware, because this plant is a highly toxic heart tonic).

right: **Dream pedlar, Florence Mary Anderson, 1914, British**
The daisy is more than merely decorative, it protects against fairy mischief.

Snowdrop Said to have materialized when the prince beloved by fairy king Oberon's daughter was slaughtered by her father. The herb she used to revive her lover transformed to a bunch of snowdrops. A bunch in a kitchen windowsill purifies the home of bad spirits.

Ferns Favored haunt of pixies. Sit on a fern, wait long enough, and you will be rewarded with sight of a fairy The moonwort fern is renowned for being able to open locks and remove the shoes from horses. Fern seed is thought to be under the jurisdiction of Oberon: it makes the owner invisible. It also offers the power of divination in love matters.

Cowslip Associated with springtime, these flowers have the power to confer beauty and act as a sedative. They may offer up the secret location of fairy gold, like forget-me-nots. Fairies are said to take flight within the flowers (Fairy Cups) on spying danger, and to use them as umbrellas in rain.

That they do dwell within the cowslips hollow is truth for I have seen them fly out in intoxicated abandon.

EDMUND CANTERBELL

left: **Cowslips, Walter Crane, from *Flowers from Shakespeare's Garden,* 1906, British**
These golden flowers are thought to resemble the shape of a cow's lips.

All the names I know from nurse:
Gardener's garters,
  Shepherd's purse,
Bachelor's buttons, Lady's smock,
And the Lady Hollyhock.

Fairy places, fairy things,
Fairy woods where the wild
  bee wings,
Tiny trees for tiny dames—
These must all be fairy names!

Tiny woods below whose boughs
Shady fairies weave a house;
Tiny tree-tops, rose or thyme,
Where the braver fairies climb!

Fair are grown-up people's trees,
But the fairest woods are these;
Where if I were not so tall,
I should live for good and all.

ROBERT LOUIS STEVENSON

Thorn, Ash and Oak are their favorite trees
So perhaps you could circle the boughs with these:
Some Foxgloves for thimbles, some Thyme for a treat
Bluebells for their magic and logs for a seat!
Plant Primrose and eat them if you dare by the day
and it is said by the evening you'll glance a few Fey!

Believe in the fairies who make dreams come true.
Believe in the magic from the fairies above,
They dance in the flowers and sing songs of love.
And if you believe and always stay true,
The fairies will be there to watch over you.

GRIMSHAW

I am off down the road
Where the fairy lanterns glowed
And the little pretty flitter-mice are flying
A slender band of gray
It runs creepily away
And the hedges and the grasses are a-sighing.
The air is full of wings,
And of blundery beetle-things
That warn you with their whirring and
their humming.
O! I hear the tiny horns
Of enchanged leprechauns
And the padded feet of many gnomes a-coming!
O! the lights! o! the gleams! O! the little twinkly
    sounds!
O! the rustle of their noiseless little robes!
O! the echo of their feet – of their happy little
    feet!
O! the swinging lamps in the starlit globes.

J.R. TOLKIEN

chapter 9
Meeting the Fay

There may be fairies at the bottom of the garden. There is no evidence for it, but you can't prove that there aren't any, so shouldn't we be agnostic with respect to fairies?

RICHARD DAWKINS

previous page: **Helga and Sigurd, H.J. Ford, Andrew Lang's *Crimson Fairy Book,* 1903, British**

right: **In the Fairy Ring, Florence Harrison, c. 1910, British**

A child gazes down at a ring of fairies as they surround her in a dance.

Enticing wives and lovers

Fairies generally lead an autonomous life in their enchanted underground or underwater palaces—independent fairy courts are overseen by kings and queens and attended by servants, while there are fairy markets for trading, revels, and fairs for recreation. But fairyland still needs replenishment from human stock. Most often this is reflected in changeling stories, but fairy folk are always on the lookout for pretty maids and handsome men to serve as consorts to royalty. Ireland's fairy queen Onagh, wife to Finvarra, is more beautiful than any fairy in her silver robe studded with brilliants and hair of spun gold brushing the ground. But even so, her king prefers mortal women, who he entices from their homes with music.

left: **The fairies go off with the farmer's wife, H J Ford, *The Lilac Fairy Book*, Andrew Lang, 1919, British**
This Irish tale is a classic example of how an unsuspecting young woman is abducted by the fairies for their own ends.

She is the Sky-woman of the Dawn … She is the light on the foam. She is white and odorous as an apple-blossom. She smells of spice and honey. She is my beloved beyond the women of the world. She shall never be taken from me.

JAMES STEPHENS, *IRISH FAIRY TALES*

right: **The fairy Saeve, Arthur Rackham, from James Stephens, *Irish Fairy Tales,* 1920, British**

The Irish folk hero Fionn falls in love with Saeve, the bewitching fairy woman who begs him to protect her from her tormentors.

Fairy-human intermingling

The love affair between humans and fairies goes two ways, producing fascinating results by way of "halfling" creatures, and imaginatively spicing up the human gene pool in the process. Interbreeding with fairies is relatively common in folk stories, and usually it involves making a deal with the other world. In a Welsh tale, *The Shepherd of Myddvai* wins a lake maiden with a gift of bread. They marry, with the agreement that he will not strike her—a common bargaining tool in stories of this nature. They enjoy a family life and children, but come the inevitable blow, the fairy wife and mother departs. Sometimes, the fairy bride (or father) passes on something of the supernatural for posterity: webbed hands or feet, scaly skin, the gift of second sight or of healing. Even today, Welsh healers trace their inheritance to lake-fairy brides, while old Scottish and Irish families trace theirs to Merrow partnerships.

And there may be tangible evidence, also. Fairy cups exist, and in Dunvegan Castle on Skye one can view the Fairy Flag, a fragment of fabric torn by a chieftain of the MacLeods from his fairy wife's cape or robe as she returned to her fairy hill. The flag brings help to its descendants in times of need. Other families have been adopted by a fairy cousin down the generations: a fully fairy offspring of the fairy parent (they live for generations) who warns, helps avert danger and provides other supernatural aid.

The fairy-human connection goes back beyond historically recorded time. Many sources have speculated on whether mankind's accounts of fairies stem from early modern man's folk memories of older races on the verge of extinction, such as cave-dwelling Neanderthals. The discovery in 2004 on the Indonesian island Flores of a dwarf species of human who lived alongside modern humans fueled the speculation (and injected new themes into fantasy novels and gaming). Having the stature of a three-year-old, the new species was nicknamed "the hobbit."

Controversial archaeologist Margaret Murray equated legends of fairies in Europe with incidents of modern humans meeting shorter, stockier pre-Indo-European peoples. Others suggest that fairies might be folk memories of tribes on the boundaries of settled communities. Fairy lore gives its own account that might seem to support such theories. The trooping fairies of Ireland, the *Daoine Sidhe*, are said to be the original inhabitants of the islands, the *Tuatha dé Danaan,* driven underground by conquering races. Certainly, folklore has always insisted that belief in fairies is nearing extinction. We say this today as the poet Chaucer did seven centuries ago, and as the "Once Upon a Time" device distances literary fairy tales to an updateable past.

... you must never strike me with iron: if you do, I must be free to leave you and return to my family

W. JENKYN THOMAS *THE WELSH FAIRY BOK*

left: **Andrew King and the Fairy Wife, Arthur Rackham, from *The Book of Pictures,* 1913, British**

Once the forbidden blow has been struck, the fairy wife will depart forever.

Protective metal

However many romantic tales there are of human-fay romance and passion, human beings have also experienced the counterbalancing emotion of fear. That's why mankind has amassed an armory of defenses to disarm fairies, ranging from from making jokes to ringing them away with bells. The most reliable seem to involve metal: you only need to think of the brave prince wielding his trusty sword to cut through the impenetrable thicket surrounding Sleeping Beauty, the innocent victim of malicious fairy enchantment.

Iron and steel provide the most consistent protection against fairies of all genres and locales. In parts of West Africa it is efficient simply to repeat the word "iron" out loud several times, though in other parts of West Africa it is items made from bronze and brass that are trustingly relied upon for their protective power. From brass, too, came charms that kept a British working horse, and centuries later houses and pubs, safely ornamented.

In Norway, silver is talismanic: women might pin on a silver brooch to protect against spirits, which recharges each Sunday in church. Silver is important in the Islamic world, too, associated with the Prophet Muhammad, and tarnishes if not attended to daily, like the soul without prayer. Needles and pins are effective for being menacingly pointed as well as metallic; scissors and knives also carry the reputation for being able to "cut" relationships, when handed from one person to another. Tuck them into a pocket when venturing into places of danger, such as forests. In Morocco, one might wear a tiny dagger for fighting the Djinn alongside a miniature candle by which to find them.

How to use it

Nail a horseshoe to the door: it must be found on the ground. Horseshoes bring with them the protection of the crescent moon they resemble.

Hang up horse brasses: look for bell, sun, and heart motifs.

Triple charm house keys: attach them, using red cord, to a stone naturally bored with a hole.

Protect a room: place metal implements under the bed and above windows; lean a poker against the chimney breast.

Wear a metal ring, or belt with a metal buckle: the magic of a circle is strengthened when it contains an element of metal. If you have no metal, chalk a circle and step inside, or lure the spirit inside.

Wear some silver: place a cross around the neck or coin in the shoe.

I jest to Oberon, and make him smile
When I a fat and bean-fed horse beguile,
Neighing in likeness of a filly foal ...

WILLIAM SHAKESPEARE, *A MIDSUMMER NIGHT'S DREAM*

right: **Horse wearing protective brasses, cigarette card, 1923, British**
Brass talismans have long been favored by English countryfolk to protect
their horses from abduction by fairies, and for general good luck.

Holy words

In Catholic communities in particular, fairies have an anaphylactic reaction to signs of the Christian faith. The making of a cross and the saying of a prayer disturb them when out and about, particularly if you aim the crossing action at the spirit, in effect dissecting him. In Norway one is urged to carry a sliver from the church wall as a protective charm (never let such charms touch the ground or they lose their power). On lonely paths wayside crosses deter the bad and protect those who pass places of supernatural power. In the home, it's best to keep open a copy of the Bible and fix up a crucifix.

The portable cross on a chain is especially powerful against spirits because it is made from talismanic metal; crucifixes made by a blacksmith accrue some of his magic powers. The cross has protective influence not only in Christian cultures: the amuletic three-legged triskel in the Celtic world and the four-legged swastika in India have the effect of thrusting malevolent forces out from their whirling centers, and their extending ray motifs recall the benevolent power of the sun. In Hindu homes, bad spirits are kept out by depictions of Vishnu and Shiva. In Muslim communities the hand of Fatima halts all.

left: **The fairy bride departs, unknown artist, from Collin de Plancy's** *Legendes des Esprits,* **1862, French**
As soon as the fairy wife hears the name of God mentioned, she is compelled to leave her human husband.

A true heart

Goodness is often rewarded in tales of fairies: stay simple, true, and honest and you are more likely to survive an encounter with the fay. Bold love catches back those altered by enchantment. This is best exemplified in the ballad of Tam Lin, a compendium of Scottish fairy understanding. A young woman, Janet, finds herself pregnant by an elfin knight. She confronts him to find out what he is and how she might be with him. He explains that he is a man transformed and how she must grasp him as he rides through the sky on Hallowe'en, and keep hold, fearing not as the fairy magic warps him from state to elemental state: fierce creatures, red-hot iron, burning lead, and finally naked man. The ballad is at turns chilling, exhilarating, and cheering. Above all it celebrates the power of a feisty woman, for she who knows what's right and has a fiercely loyal heart triumphs over the forces of the other.

Then he appeared in her arms
Like the wolf that neer woud tame;
She held him fast, let him not go,
Case they neer meet again.
Then he appeared in her arms
Like the fire burning bauld;
She held him fast, let him not go,
He was as iron cauld.
And he appeared in her arms

Like the adder an the snake;
She held him fast, let him not go,
He was her warld's make.
And he appeared in her arms
Like to the deer sae wild;
She held him fast, let him not go,
He's father o' her child.
And he appeared in her arms
Like to a silken string;
She held him fast, let him not go,
Till she saw fair morning.
And he appeared in her arms
Like to a naked man;
She held him fast, let him not go,
And wi her he's gane hame.

FRANCIS JAMES CHILD *TAM LIN IN THE ENGLISH AND SCOTTISH POPULAR BALLADS*

Human wiles

Some fairy creatures are exceedingly dim-witted, and can easily be out-foxed by a thoughtful human. Confuse and disorientate is one option. This is done quite easily by turning your coat inside out, putting it on back to front, placing left shoe on right foot, and so on. If you meet a stranger in the woods, stand in his track but facing away from him. This spellbinds a silly spirit, as does running backward, staring the creature in the eyes.

Trolls, like other northern European spirits of forest and mountains, detest human noise: toddlers whining, pans clanging, saws whirring keep them away. Or wind them up for furious revenge. What spirits hate most is the ringing of church bells, which banish the most persistent. At other times, it works best to keep quiet. If you have been away with the fairies or spied one, do not boast of it. The Cherokee say that death comes not after spending time in fairyland, but on speaking of the *Yunwi Djunsti* who dwell there. Here's how to deal with fairy trouble:

• Travelers caught abroad tend to be alone. When venturing into new areas after dark, take along a well-known companion (not a smooth-talking man or one who jingles with tell-tale bells).
• Keep your wits about you, and note what is said and unsaid. Not until you ask the right question can you hope to find a name revealed.
• Throw something: your left shoe, a handful of soil (from a molehill); to pick it up, fairies drop whatever they are holding—it might be your wife.
• Cross-roads can disorientate spirits (though they also lurk here).
• Look for the obvious fatal flaw. In Latin America it might show as some kind of strangeness about the knees; other spirits might have a tail or

hairy feet peeping from otherwise elegant attire. Keep a watchful eye.

• Be assured that some fairies—the Welsh among them—have an innate sense of the just (not for nothing are some known as the fair ones) and stick to the letter of an agreement, even if it results in destruction.

• Tell a joke. Mischievous spirits like to laugh and it disarms them; but it has to be a good one.

Some of the Trolls are very stupid, and there are many stories as to how they have been outwitted … A farmer ploughed a hill-side field. Out came a Troll and said, "What do you mean by plowing up the roof of my house?" Then the farmer, being frightened, begged his pardon, but said it was a pity such a fine piece of land should lie idle. The Troll agreed to this, and then they struck a bargain that the farmer should till the land and that each of them should share the crops. One year the Troll was to have, for his share, what grew above ground, and the next year what grew underground. So in the first year the farmer sowed carrots, and the Troll had the tops; and the next year the farmer sowed wheat, and the Troll had the roots; and the story says he was very well content.

JOHN THACKRAY BUNCE *FAIRY TALES; THEIR ORIGIN AND MEANING WITH SOME ACCOUNT OF DWELLERS IN FAIRYLAND*

Fairy muses

With the nineteenth century came a flourishing of fairy-inspired music from European composers inspired by national folklore and folk tunes, and by the Romantic obsession with wild nature and the supernatural. Composers were drawn by the Gothic darkness of troll stories or, pulled in another direction, were enthralled by fairy muses, who they set on stage in blocked *pointe* shoes and billowing gauze, flesh and blood incarnations of other-worldly figures who inspire a poet to great work, but ultimately destroy him.

A trip to the theater or concert hall offered a thrilling refuge from an increasingly mechanized urban world, where one would be transported by spine-tingling unease, echoes of a simpler age, and the dazzling vision of perfect accomplishment. Might there be a link with the flowering of new age faery in a world where technology tracks our every movement, overloads us with information and trivia, and ensures no escape from the deadline? The lure of a more frothy but also more dangerous world, where imagination and desire rule, nothing is quite as it should be, and roles and edges blur, is most alluring.

left: Carlotta Grisi, unattributed engraving, 1841, Italian
The Italian ballet dancer was famous for her interpretation of *Giselle*.

Must-hear fairy music

Overture to Oberon by Carl Maria von Weber: from the father of the Romantic movement in music, this overtures carries the listener from fairyland to mermaid's cave.

Peer Gynt by Edvard Grieg: thrill to *March of the Trolls* and I*n the Hall of the Mountain King* and hear the sparkling Norwegian forest.

La Sylphide by Jean Schneitzhoeffer: ballet set in Scotland in which a bridegroom falls in love with a winged sylph. Try Matthew Bourne's gritty modern take: the hero is deranged and destroyed by an unattainable new-age fairy.

The Nutcracker Suite by Peter Tchaikovsky: premiered in 1892, this ballet's sugar-plum fairies have become the epitome of Christmas dance.

Rusalka by Antonin Dvorak: opera based on the fairy temptress from the water first performed in 1901 in Prague.

Les Sylphides by Frédéric Chopin: with no plot, this ballet, first performed by the Ballets Russes, is a "romantic reverie" set in a moonlit park: the sylphs embody the forces of poetic inspiration and creation.

Ondine by Hans Werne Henze: Frederick Ashton's ballet for his muse Margot Fonteyn, who played the temptress water sprite of the title, premiered in 1958. Compare the vivid, lyrical score with Debussy's piano prelude and Ravel's work of the same name.

right: The dance, H. J. Ford from Andrew Lang's *The Lilac Fairy Book*, 1919, British
A bewitching dancing maiden frolics with sea creatures and a young man playing bagpipes.

For the true explanation of these fairy photographs what is wanted is not a knowledge of occult phenomena, but a knowledge of children.

FROM *TRUTH* NEWSPAPER, 1917

left: **Frances Griffiths and the fairy taken by Elsie Wright, from *The Coming of the Fairies,* Sir Arthur Conan Doyle, 1922, British**
Frances and Elsie made such a persuasive team of fairy observers, they even convinced the inventor of Sherlock Holmes.

The Cottingley mystery

A set of photographs was the fairy sensation of the early twentieth century. Cousins Frances Griffiths and Elsie Wright, aged 11 and 16, claimed to have encountered fairies in their garden—and had prints to prove it. The images, shot in 1917, showed the girls with tiny dancing figures, who they claimed were fairies of the beck, or stream, even though they resembled modern-looking figures from Parisian style books. In the first photographs Frances stared at the camera through a vision of prancing winged creatures; Elsie held out a hand for a grotesque winged gnome to perch on. It wasn't until 1919 that the pictures were picked up outside the family, after Elsie's mother attended a meeting of the Theosophical Society, some of whose members studied fairy lore.

By 1920, leading Theosophist Edward Gardner had commissioned sharp prints from the negatives, and they finally were submitted to public scrutiny. After initial skepticism, many figures of authority seemed convinced of their authenticity, including Spiritualist Arthur Conan Doyle, creator of Sherlock Holmes. A firm believer in "dwellers at the border," he wrote up the girls' story for the Christmas 1920 edition of *The Strand* magazine, and with Gardner, commissioned more photographs. The public went wild, and the paper sold out in days. The girls captured three more images using Gardner's equipment: a figure offering harebells, a fairy bower, published in 1921, also in *The Strand,* and one last, more mysterious blurred exposure of floating fairy forms.

The cousins kept their counsel over the decades, teasing the tabloid and TV reporters who sought them out. It was not until 1983, aged 76, that Frances admitted what many had suspected: the figures in the first four photographs had been faked by the girls. But in a surprisingly low-tech, child-friendly way. It was not trick photography, as commentators, including Kodak, had surmised, but that favorite girlhood pastime, cutting and sticking. Illustrations from the 1914 *Princess Mary's Gift Book* (a Conan Doyle story appeared in the same edition) were snipped out, suspended on hat pins, and photographed with a borrowed camera. In the second round of images, the figures were hung from branches. However, the last photograph, of "fairies building up in the grasses," Frances claimed, had not been faked, but proved what the girls swore to their deaths: there *were* fairies in this spot.

I went off, too, to Cottingley again, taking the two cameras and plates from London, and met the family and explained to the two girls the simple working of the cameras, giving one each to keep. The cameras were loaded, and my final advice was that they need go up to the glen only on fine days as they had been accustomed to do before and 'tice the fairies, as they called their way of attracting them, and see what they could get. I suggested only the most obvious and easy precautions about lighting and distance, for I knew it was essential they should feel free and unhampered and have no burden of responsibility. If nothing came of it all, I told them, they were not to mind a bit.

EDWARD L. GARDNER, *FAIRIES: A BOOK OF REAL FAIRIES*

**Come fairies
take me out of this dull world,
for I would ride with you
upon the wind and dance
upon the mountains like a flame.**

W.B. YEATS

right: **A fairy on a fingertip, Claude Shepperson from *Princess Mary's Gift Book,* c. 1915, British**

Fairies bring enchantment to our world—that's why we seek them.

If you want your children to be intelligent, read them fairy tales. If you want them to be more intelligent, read them more fairy tales.

ALBERT EINSTEIN

left: **A falling star, from *Elfin Song*, Florence Harrison, 1912, British**
Every child needs to use his or her imagination to explore unknown realms through the pathways of fairytale.

Why we need to believe

If we need meetings with fairies to teach us gifts of healing and spirituality, we need them also to inspire the imagination, entertain, chill, and edify. Charles Dickens believed that, "In a utilitarian age, of all other times, it is a matter of grave importance that fairy tales should be respected." C. S. Lewis, too, valued fantasy worlds, which by their definition cannot be "true," for allowing us experiences we might never have in the world of the possible. In the introduction to his 1956 volume, *Italian Folktales,* Italo Calvino describes how during his two-year immersion in the project, the world took on "the attributes of fairyland."

He saw spells and transformation in the most everyday occurrences and humans began to exhibit fairy characteristics, apt to disappear or act enchanted. He realized that the rules of fairyland are "a general explanation of life." Important though it is to tune in to fairies at every life stage, it is most vital that we raise our children to believe; getting the habit young of looking beyond the material realm matters.

Being open to worlds in which grown ups have little investment liberates, empowers, and is necessary to mental health. Having the faith to keep believing in something that is at its essence unknowable, and feeling content in the presence of contradictions is soul-expanding. Exploring unknown worlds through words and in paint, music and movement, and storytelling keeps magical worlds of possibilities alive. Here are some places to start.

Fairy books for children

The Golden Book of Fairy Tales by Marie Ponsot and Adrienne Segur: an American classic translated from the French.

The Book of Little Folk by Lauren Mills: key collection of tales and poems from around the world.

Flower Fairies of the Spring/Summer/Autumn/Winter by Cicely Mary Barker: enchanting for even the youngest tots.

The Winter Child by Terri Windling and Wendy Froud: the picture-book adventures of a tree-root fairy with images by doll-artist Wendy Froud.

Finn Family Moomintroll by Tove Jansson: a treasury of troll stories from one of the 20th-century's finest children's writers.

The Borrowers by Mary Norton: from the same era as the Moomims, English wee folk (are they fairies?) who live beneath the hearth.

The Lion, the Witch and the Wardrobe by C. S. Lewis: remains the most memorable literary portal into an other world; pay attention to the tree spirits.

The Owl Service by Alan Garner: for older children, a haunting tale based on Welsh mythology.

The Dark is Rising by Susan Cooper: superlative magic series for older readers.

The Wee Free Men by Terry Pratchett: spine-chilling and hilarious by turns: all fairy lore is here.

Growing Wings by Laurel Winter: an 11-year old sprouts wings; this is her story.

Fairy books for adults

Lady Cottington's Pressed Fairy Book by Brian Froud: a classic of fairy magic and mayhem now in a 10 3/4 anniversary edition.

Fairie-ality: the fashion collection from The House of Ellwand: fairy couture collections for every season and occasion crafted from feathers, leaves, and petals. Rose petal mules on a birch-bark sole with cow parsley seed trim anyone?

The Bloody Chamber by Angela Carter: ravishing, haunting, and influential retellings of tales that stay with you for ever.

Kingdoms of Elfin by Sylvia Townsend Warner: unassailable stories of faeries living on the edges of our world; out of print but findable online.

The Wood Wife, Terri Windling: engaging mythic novel from a human hub of the fairy world.

The Truth about Celia by Kevin Brockmeier: chilling interwoven stories about a daughter who disappears to fairyland.

Jonathan Strange and Mr Norrell by Susannah Clarke: described as Jane Austen with fairies; fantastic footnotes.

Spirits in the Wires by Charles de Lint: brings to life the spirits who inhabit phones and the internet.

Tam Lin by Pamela Dean: the essential fairy ballad set in a modern background.

Thomas the Rhymer by Ellen Kushner: romantic retelling of a ballad of abduction by an elfin queen.

Fairies in the movies

Those who have grown up since the second half of the twentieth century have a new thread from which to weave our understanding of fairies. The films of Walt Disney scatter snatches of sparkling fairy lore over diverse global cultures just as Tinkerbell's magic wand sprinkles fairy dust over the opening of a classic Disney movie. The combination of movement, color, speech, and music lends itself to stories of magical transformation, and must have seemed like fairy wizardry at the dawn of animation. It continues to transport us to other worlds. In the tradition of the ever-warping fairytale, which molds in every new century to fit a new audience, so bit players from fairy tales such as Cinderella's fairy godmother, the *Little Mermaid*, the seven dwarves, Pinocchio's blue fairy, and the fortune fairies have had their pasts whipped away from them and their roles magnified.

Take Tinkerbell, Peter Pan's companion from the J. M. Barrie stories; she underwent a magical transformation in 2005 with the launch of an unprecedented $1 million marketing campaign to build a multi-billion dollar franchise around her. Tinkerbell is the first Disney brand to be established without a movie. Disney research shows that Tinkerbell has a high recognition factor among young girls (around 90 per cent), way out of proportion with her non-speaking role in the 1953 film *Peter Pan*. Petite "Tink," who is sassy and brave states the Disney fairy site, is fiercely loyal to her friends, and terrifying to those who wish them ill, but we forgive everything when she flashes that dimpled smile.

Elves and brownies

When Agnes and Olave Baden-Powell set up the Girl Guide Association in the early years of the twentieth century they chose the role model of little folk who help around the home for their younger sisters, Brownie Guides—girls aged between seven and ten. They adapted a story first published in 1879 by Mrs Juliana Ewing, a favorite children's author, whose imaginative language and bold humor influenced a generation of children's writers. The Brownie tale uses the motifs of the wise owl (a common form for shape-shifting spirits), scrying in a mirror-like pool of water, toadstools, incantation, and wisdom hidden deep in the woods.

Until recently Brownie Guides held their promise ceremony (initiation into the group) standing in a ring around a toadstool and looking glass, repeating some of the magical incantation. Elements of the story and theme remain today. Brownie leaders take the name of an owl (Brown Owl, Tawny, Snowy) and the girls divide into groups (or sixes) that may be named after fairy folk: elves, sprites, imps, *ghillie dhu*. But other elements of the Brownie story (the toadstool and mirror) have been excluded from Brownie activities, or updated to suit modern taste. Sixes, for example, are now as likely to be named for those other night terrors of country life, the fox, badger, and mole. But novice Brownies from around the world still read a Brownie Story adapted from Mrs. Ewing.

left: **The owl and the grasshopper, Charles Folkard, Aesop's *Fables*, 1912, British**
The wise owl is the favored emblem of Brownie leaders.

The Brownie Story

The cottage on the edge of the wood was in an awful mess. There were dishes to be washed, clothes to be ironed and toys scattered all over the floor. Tommy and Betty didn't care. They hated boring old housework. "What I am going to do?" their mother sighed. "I can't keep the cottage tidy. If only we had a Brownie!" "What's a Brownie?" asked Tommy. "A Brownie is a magical little creature, which slips into houses very early before anyone is awake. It tidies toys, irons clothes, washes dishes and does all sorts of helpful things in secret," replied his mother.

"That's great! How can we get one?" wondered Betty. "The Wise Owl in the wood would know I suppose," her mother said. Late that night, Tommy and Betty crept out of the cottage into the wood. It was cold and dark and full of shadows. Or were they ghosts? "We can't go back. We've got to find the Wise Owl," said Betty firmly. "Twitt twoo. How do you do?" a voice hooted at them from a nearby tree. "The Wise Owl!" Tommy hugged Betty in relief.

And soon the children were seated on a branch snuggling close to the big bird's feathers. They explained they were looking for a Brownie. "Do you know where we could find one?" asked Betty. "Indeed I do hooted the Owl, and, placing her beak close to Betty's ear, she explained. "Tommy, imagine!" exclaimed Betty. "There's a Brownie in that pool over there. I've got to go to the pool over there. I've got to turn round three times and say:

"Twist me and turn me and show me the elf, I looked in the water and there saw…".' "Who? Who? Who?" hooted the Owl. "Look into the water and you'll find your Brownie looking back at you. Her name will finish the rhyme. The children raced over to the pool. Betty did exactly as the Owl had said: "Twist me and turn me and show me the elf, I looked in the water and there saw…" She looked into the pool. "Well, can you see it? Can you see a Brownie?" yelled Tommy, hopping from foot to foot in excitement. "No," said Betty, All I can see is my own reflection." Tommy and Betty were so tired and disappointed that by the time they reached the tree again, they were in tears. "Boo, hoo, hoo. What's the matter with you two?" hooted the Owl, offering them a hanky. "We didn't find a Brownie," sniffed Betty. "I saw no one in the water but myself." "Well, well" said the Owl. "Let's see if that fits the rhyme." "Twist me and turn me and show me the elf, I looked in the water and there saw…" "Myself!" finished Betty. "But I'm not a Brownie!" "Too true, too true," hooted the Owl. "But you could act like one for a change and so could Tommy. It would be fun."

Tommy and Betty returned thoughtfully to the cottage. If you had passed that way very early next morning, you would have seen a lamp burning in the kitchen window and two figures busily scurrying about inside. And when the children's mother came down for breakfast, she couldn't believe her eyes. There wasn't a toy in sight. Everything was clean and tidy. "Why, a Brownie has been here. How wonderful!" she gasped.

From that day to this, the cottage has been a different place. And Tommy and Betty have been like different children. They never get bored now; they are too busy planning their secret good turns. Of course, their mother has discovered the truth. She thinks she is very lucky to have such helpful children. And Tommy and Betty have discovered how right the Wise Owl was: being human Brownies is FUN!

ADAPTED FROM *THE BROWNIES* BY MRS. EWING 1ST BURLEY-IN-WHARFEDALE BROWNIES, YORKSHIRE, ENGLAND

Some say no evil thing that walks by night,
In fog or fire, by lake or moorish fen,
Blue meagre hag, or stubborn unlaid ghost
That breaks his magic chains at curfew time,
No goblin, or swart fairy of the mine,
Hath hurtful power o'er true virginity …

JOHN MILTON

The islanders, like all the Irish, believe that the fairies are the fallen angels who were cast down by the Lord God out of heaven for their sinful pride. And some fell into the sea, and some on the dry land, and some fell deep down into hell, and the devil gives to these knowledge and power, and sends them on earth where they work much evil.

LADY WILDE

This is Mab, the mistress Fairy,
That doth nightly rob the dairy,
And can help or hurt the churning,
As she please without discerning.
She that pinches country wenches,
If they rub not clean their benches,
And with sharper nails remembers
When they rake not up their embers:
But if so they chance to feast her,
In a shoe she drops a tester.
This is she that empties cradles,
Takes out children, puts in ladles:
Trains forth midwives in their slumber,
With a sieve the holes to number …

BEN JONSON

Web resources

Websites

www.endicott-studio.com Inspiring essays on fairy themes under the editorship of the great Terri Windling. Great recommendations for fairy literature and art.

www.surlalunefairytales.com The best web resource for fairy tale scholarship, with expert contributors, fascinating message boards, and invaluable annotated fairy tales.

www.sacred-texts.com A "quiet place in cyberspace devoted to religious tolerance and scholarship" where you can browse collections of Celtic, Norse, and European tales and folklore.

www.pitt.edu/~dash/ashliman.html The best online site for academically sifted European folk and fairy tales, arranged by theme, with new translations from Professor D. L. Ashliman of the University of Pittsburgh.

www.loc.gov/folklife The American folklife center at The Library of Congress.

www.orkneyjar.com Folklore and fairies of the Orkney Islands.

www.cornishfolklore.com The Cornish Folklore Society, trying to establish a living tradition of storytelling.

ww.irelandseye.com/leprechaun Home to Leprechaun watch: a web cam sited in a fairy tree overlooking a fairy ring in Tipperary. You are urged to report sightings.

www.worldoffroud.com Essential for Froudians, the headquarters of Brian and Wendy Froud's fairy art.

www.flowerfairies.com Official site of Cicely Mary Barker's classic *Flower Fairies.*

wwww.io.com/~fazia/Moomin.html Tove Jansson's *Moomintroll* home pages.

www.emmadavies.net Find your fairy name. Great fun.

www.toothfairys.net Traditions from around the world.

www.mouseplanet.com/fairytales Fascinating look at Disney's take on fairy stories.

www.freethegnomes.com For information on Garden Gnome Liberation and calls to action. "We advocate an end to oppressive gardening and freedom for garden gnomes everywhere."

www.feeverte.net Everything you could ever want to know about la *fée verte,* absinthe.

http://disney.go.com/fairies Meet Tinkerbell, who hosts this site and introduces her new fairy friends.

Bibliography

Collections of Tales

The Fairy-Faith in Celtic Countries, W. Y. Evans-Wentz, 1911

Ancient Legends, Mystic Charms, and Superstitions of Ireland, Lady
    Francesca Speranza Wilde, 1887

Legendary Fictions of the Irish Celts, Patrick Kennedy, 1866

Irish Fairy Tales, James Stephens, 1920

Folk-Lore and Legends, Scotland, W. W. Gibbings, 1889

*The Popular Superstitions and Festive Amusements of the Highlanders
    of Scotland,* W. Grant Stewart, 1823

The English and Scottish Popular Ballads, Francis James Child,
    1882–98

The Welsh Fairy Book, W. Jenkyn Thomas, 1908

*British Goblins: Welsh Folk-lore, Fairy Mythology, Legends and
    Traditions,* Wirt Sikes, 1880

Popular Romances of the West of England, Robert Hunt, 1871

Popular Tales from the Norse, Sir George Webbe Dasent, 1888

Songs of the Russian People, W. R. S. Ralston, 1872

European Folk and Fairy Tales, Joseph Jacobs, 1916

Household Tales, Jacob and Wilhelm Grimm, translated Margaret
    Hunt, 1884

The Blue Fairy Book, Andrew Lang, 1889

Myths and Legends of Japan, F. Hadland Davis, 1913

*The Fairy Mythology, Illustrative of the Romance and Superstition of
    Various Countries,* Thomas Keightley, 1850

*Fairy Tales; Their Origin and Meaning with Some Account of Dwellers
    in Fairyland,* John Thackray Bunce, 1878

The Brownies and Other Tales, Juliana Horatia Ewing, 1871

Commentaries on fairies

Fairies in Tradition and Literature, Katharine Briggs, 2002, Routledge

The World Guide to Gnomes, Fairies, Elves, and Other Little People, Thomas Keightley, 1978 (reprint of 1878 edition), Gramercy Books

The Oxford Companion to Fairy Tales, Jack Zipes ed., 2003, Oxford University Press

The Classic Fairy Tales, Iona and Peter Opie, 1974, Oxford University Press

Myths, Legends, and Folktales of America, David Leeming and Jake Page, 2000, Oxford University Press

The Japanese Fairy Book, Yu Theodora Ozaki, 2003, Kessinger

Amulets: a world of secret powers, charms and magic, Sheila Paine, 2004, Thames and Hudson

Spirits, Fairies, Leprechauns, and Goblins: an encyclopedia, Carol Rose, 1996, W. W. Norton

Good Faeries, Bad Faeries, Brian Froud, 2004, Pavilion Books

A Field Guide to Demons, Fairies, Fallen Angels, and Other Subversive Spirits, Carol K Mack and Dinah Mack, 1998, Owl Books

From the Beast to the Blonde: on fairytales and their tellers, Marina Warner, 1994, Chatto and Windus

Strange and Secret Peoples: Fairies and Victorian Consciousness, Carole G. Silver, 2000, Oxford University Press

Picture credits

CORBIS

POWERSTOCK

114-115

LEICESTER GALLERIES

242-243; 325 Courtesy of Peter Nahum At The Leicester Galleries,
www.leicestergalleries.com

SCIENCE AND SOCIETY LIBRARY

page 396

All other images feautured are from the private collection of the publishers,
MQ Publications Ltd.

*Every attempt has been made to contact current copyright holders of illustrative
material. Any errors or omissions will be rectified in future edition or reprints*

Index

Page numbers in *italics*
refer to illustrations

A

absinthe 233
Adhene 224
aduction *374, 375*
Aesop, *Fables 348, 408*
agricultural spirits 178-81
air (element) 34
air fairies 33-5
Albania 291, 314
Albtraum 230
alder 350
Alfheim 34
Alfs 158, 198
Allingham, William 73,
94, 111
Alven 122
amulets 314-17
Anderson, Anne 275
Anderson, Florence Mary
90, *343, 362*
Anderson, Hans Christian
76, *347*
Arnold, Matthew 30-1
ash tree 333, *340*, 341
Asturias 199
Atwell, Mabel Lucie 287
auras 89
auspicious days 139
Aztecs 90

B

babies:
care 268
fairy *64-5*
laughter 288
protective charms for
314-15

Baden-Powell, Agnes and
Olave 409
Baku 230
Bannik fairy 342
Banshee 102, *103*
baptism 290, 291
Barrie, J.M. 288, 407
barrows 36, 42
battle nymphs 33
Bayly, Thomas Haynes
197
Bean Tighe 170
Bean-sidhe 102
Béfind 291
bells 317
Bible 38, 227, 317
birch 342
birth 290-1, 295
Blacklock, Thomas
Bromley *44-5*
blackthorn 337
Blake, William 324
Blue Bird 252
blue color 314
bluebells 363
Boggarts 198, 199
Book of Kells 92
books 405-6
border guardians 205-7
boundary sites 42
Brazil 76
breath 101
Briar Rose 216, 218-19
brides *322*, 323
fairy 378, *386*
bridegrooms 323
Briggs, Katharine 97, 357
Brittany 34, 36, 72, 76,
94, 212, 291
broomsticks 122, 342, *343*

brown color 98
Browne, William 132
Brownie Guides 409
Brownies 6, 71, 78, 130,
172, 198, 410-11
Bryant, William Cullen 62
bubbles of air 122
Buchanan, Robert
Williams 268
Buckley, Arabella B. 49
Buddha 333
Bugul Noz 72
bulwands 122
Bunce, John Thackray
200, 391
burial sites 36, 42
butter 130
butterflies *88*, 90
riding on *117*, 120
Bwbach 78, 169, 170
Bwca'r Trwyn 155

C

calendar 139, 140-9
Callicantzaroi 94
camouflage 246
Canada 131
Candlemas Eve 140
Cantabria 33
Canterbell, Edmund 364
Caointeach 02
Cascorach 135
Ceffl-dwr 126
Celts 36, 42, 71, 92, 126,
131, 139, 333, 341,
350, 387
Central America 12
Chang Hsien 291
changelings *300*, 301-13,
304, 310-11, 375

charms 314-17
Chaucer, Geoffrey 379
cheese 130
Child, Francis James
    388-9
Child Rowland 48
childbirth 290-1, 295
China 34, 314
Christianity 387
Christmas Eve 141, 142,
    143, 144-5
Christmas fairy 6, 143,
    281, 353
Christmas trees 6, 353
Cinderella 184, *185*
Clare, John 63
clothes 94-9, 95, *96*
colors 97-8
courtly 98-9
magical 246
working attire 99
Cloud People 33
clouds 33, 34, 35
clover 357
Clurichaun 171
cobblers 99, 160
cock crow 112
Collins, William 227
colors 97-8
Colshorn, Carl and
    Theodor 56-7
Copland, J. *310-11*
Cornwall 71, 72, 76, 89,
    90, 98, 158, 315
Cottingley mystery 398-9
courtly costume 98-9
cowslips 364, 365
Crane, Walter 355, 365
Croker, Thomas Crofton
    99
cross 383, 387
Cruikshank, George *165*

crusher spirit 230
Curupira 76
Cyhyraeth 102

D

daemons 35
daisies *362*, 363
dancing *50-1*, 136, 240
Daoine Sidhe 379
Daoism 349, 350
Dark *Alf* 158
Dasent, George Webbe
    207
Davenant, Sir William
    234
Davis, F. Hadland 86-7
Dawkins, Richard 372
dawn 112
daystanders 112
De la Mare, Walter 129,
    234
death 290, 324
Denmark 291, 297, 315
disease 224
disguise 246
divination 283
Domovoi 76, 171, 172, 178,
    198, 230
Dormette de Poitou 297
Doyle, Sir Arthur Conan
    89, *396*, 398
Doyle, Richard *8-9, 16-
    17,* 89, *328-9*
dragonflies, riding on *121*
Drayton, Michael 116,
    121
dreams 230, 297
dryads 12, 345
Duende 76, 170-1
Duergar 98
Dulac, Edmund *185, 209*
Dunsanant, Lord 235

dusk 112
dwarves 41, *70*, 71, 78,
    98, 112, 155, 156-9

E

earth, fairies of 36-41
earth (element) 34
Egypt 90
Einstein, Albert 403
Elbe, river 122
elder 346, *347*
elecampane 356
elf fire 34
elf stroke 227
elf-shot 227
ellyllon 169
Eloko 18
elves 18-19, *19*, 68, 71,
    76, *110*, 116, 121, 131,
    160-7, *165, 168, 174-5,*
    198, 227-9, 230
Emerson, Ralph Waldo
    61, 349
enchantment 237-85
England 130
entrance fee 56
Entwhistle, Mildred *244*
Eshu 291
euphemisms 104-5
Evans-Wentz, W.Y. 93
Ewing, Mrs Juliana 409-
    11
exorcisms 309

F

Fachan 74
fairies:
anatomical oddities 74
anatomy 65-107
appearance 68
beauty 72
beginnings of 288

hairy 78
limbs 76
size 68, 71
ugly 72
Fairy Bells 356
fairy godmother 184, *185*
fairy places to visit 58
Fairy Queen *8-9*
fairy rings 53, 238, *239*, 240, *242-3*
fairy sight 273
"fairy wind" 101
fairy-pin wells 212
fairy/human connections 377-9
fairyland 46-63
farm fairies 178
Fates 291
Fatit 291
Fear Durg 78
feasting 129
feathers 86
ferns 364
festivities 38-9
finery 94-9, 95, 96
colors 97-8
Finvarra 124, 375
flowers 360-9
Folkard, Charles 202, 408
Folletti 33, 76, 122, 246
food 129-31, 152-3
Ford, H.J. 70, 75, 373, 374, 395
forest fairies 12-15
fortune fairies 291
Fossegrim 76, 248
foxgloves 363
Foyle, Kathleen 247
France 297
see also Brittany
Friedrich, Woldemar *296*
funeral fairies 324, *325*

Fusseli, Henry 230
Fylgja 324

G
Gan Ceanach 212
garden gnomes *182*, 183
Gardner, Edward L. 398, 399
Gartenzwerg 183
Germany 48, 76, 158, 183, 198, 204, 230, 265, 353
Ghana 12
Ghillie Dhu 342
Gianes 160
Gibbings, W.W. 82-3
gifts 263-7
Girl Guide Association 409
girls, young and beautiful 12
gnomes *40*, *144-5*, *180*
garden *182*, 183
Goble, Warwick:
Book of Fairy Poetry 13, *14*, *19*, *20*, *23*, *24*, *27*, *29*, *37*, *72*, *128*, *205*, *210*, *215*, *225*, *249*, *269*, *294*
Fairy Book 110, *117*, *156-7*, *253*, *271*, *292-3*
Water Babies 85, *108-9*, *236-7*, *254*, *255*, *257*, *258-9*, *261*
goblins 22, 72, 212
goodness rewarded 388-9
Graves, Robert 150, 327
Greek mythology 18, 291, 350
green color 97
green fairy 233
Griffiths, Frances *396*, 398-9

Grim 324
Grimm, Jacob and Wilhelm 41, 160, 166-7, 218-19, *262*, 263, 274, *275*, 276, 314, *336*
Grimshaw 368
Grisi, Carlotta *392*
Grogoch 98
ground ivy 357
Gruagach 78
Gruffydd ap Dafydd 342
guardian spirits 291
guardians:
    of border 205-7
    of home 169-76
Gwyllian 102

H
hag stone 53
hag-ridden 230
hairiness 78
Hallowe'en 141, 146, 283
hallucinogens 245
Harrison, Florence:
Changelings 300, 301
Elfin Song 2, *4*, *11*, *32*, *47*, *103*, 122, *123*, *134-5*, *138*, *170-1*, *173*, *177*, *178-9*, *180*, *189*, 219, 220, *222*, 223, *228*, *247*, *299*, *300*, 319, *402*
Fairy Mill 181
Man in the Moon 298, *299*
harvest 178, 181
Hawaii 276
hawthorn 333, *336*, 337
Hawthorne, Nathaniel *344*
hazel trees 334, *335*
heathland fairies *96*
Hebrides 134
Helga and Sigurd 373

helpers 153-91
herbs 354-9
Herrick, Robert 191
hidden people 36
Highland brownie 78
hill forts 36
hills 42
hillside 34
Hindus 333, 387
Hobgoblin 72
Hofberg, Herman 312-13
hollow bodies 76
Holzfrauen 19
home, guardians of 169-76
Hood, Thomas 280, 284
Hopkins, Gerard Manley 285
horse brasses 383, *385*
horsemen 124-5
horses 124-5, 126, *127*, 248-9
horseshoes 383
house spirits 71, 169-76, 198
pleasing 176
house-goblin *155*
Housman, A.E. 151
Hrist 33
Hughes, Edward Robert *52*, 53, *325*
Hulderfolk 36
Huldra 104, 291
human wiles 390-1
Hun, Robert 226

I
Iceland 198, 324
imagination 404
Imbolc 140
imps *77*, *196*, *250*
incubus 230

India 56, 387
Indonesia 378-9
invisibility 246
Ireland 36, 68, 78, 92, 98, 102, 124-5, 135, 170, 171, 246, 309, 333, 337, 379
iron 381, 382
Islam (Muslims) 317, 387
Italy 33, 76, 94, 97, 122, 160, 246, 314

J
Japan 33, 86-7, 230, 314, 350
Jonson, Ben 107, 143, 284
Judaism 89

K
kanashibari 230
Katha Upanishad 332
Kauffmann, 152-3
Keats, John 213-14
Keilig, Karl *80-1*
Kelpies 126, 249
Kennedy, Patrick 272
keys 383
killcrop 309
Kilmeny *13*
Kingsley, Charles *85*, *108-9*, *236-7*, *254*, 255-6, *257*, *258-9*, 260, *261*
Kirk, Robert 34, 35, 122, 130-1, 139, 164, 324
Knockers 71, 158
knowes 36
Kobold 76, 199
Korea 264
Korrigan 212

L
lairs, finding 42
Land of Promise 46
Landon, L.E. 22
Lang, Andrew 106, 156, 161, 186-8, *373*, *374*, *395*
Langsuir 76
Latino tales 76
Latvia 204
laughter:
of babies 288
spirit 102
Leal da Camara, Thomas Julio *231*
Lenihan, Eddie 337
Lennon, John 60
Leprechauns 71, *72*, 73, 97, 160, 199, 264
Lhiannan-shee 208
light, beings of 92-3
limbs 76
Lithuania 176, 204
Livemont, Privat *232*
Ljósálfar 34
Loireag 134
Lorioux, Félix *95*, *120*
Lughnasadh 140
Luhmann, Baz 233
Luminous Ones 92
Lunantishee fairies 337
Luther, Martin 309
Lyeshy 15
Lyktgubbe 34
Lyly, John 224

M
Mab, Queen 66, 116, 191, 413
MacCrimmons family 136
Mack, Lizzie (Lawson) *281*

Macleod, Fiona 326
Malaysia 18, 76
Malino 199
Mami Wata 97
Man in the Moon 298, *299*
Manx tales 208, 224
Maoris 90, 92, 131
Mara 230
marriage 290
marshland 34
Marui 160
May Day/Eve 140, 337, 346
Mbulu 101
mer people 74
Mer-men 21, 212
Meredith, George 10
Mermaids 21, *24*, 25, *75*, 82-3, 101, 102, 357
Merrow 102, 246
metal, protective 382-3
midnight 112
Midsummer Day/Eve *52*, 53, 140, 283, 341, 345, 357
milk 130
Milton, John 295, 412
miners 41, *70*, 99
Minogue, Kylie 233
mischief-makers 193-235
Mist 33
mistletoe 345
Mona Ciello 97
Moore, Clement Clarke 142
moorland fairies 98
Moreau, Gustave *100*
Morgan ap Rhys 265, 266-7
moths 90
Moulin Rouge (film) 233
mounds 42

mountains 36
movies 407
mugwort 357
Murray, Amelia Jane *118-19*
Murray, Margaret 379
muryans 71, 98-9
music 132-6
fairy-inspired 393-4
Muslims (Islam) 317, 387

N

Näcken 102, 136, 249
names 104-5
secret 276-9
Native Americans 33, 90, 276, 349, 350
Nautilus 22, *23*
ndoki 309
Neanderthals 378
New Year's Eve 141
Newfoundland 227, 230
Nicholas, St 142
Nigeria 291
night-time mischief 230
nightmares 230
Nisse 142, 199, 200, *201*
Nixies 21
Norse myths 33, 34, 71, 158, 341
North Wind Fairy 32
Norway 36, 76, 104, 248, 291, 382, 387
November Eve 146, 147-9
Nucklelavees 89
nursery spirits *296*, 297

O

oak 333, *344*, 345
Oberon *114-15*, *270*, 303, 305, *358*, 360
O'Carolan, Turlough 136
Odysseus 102

ointment 38, 272-3
Old Close Your Eyes 297
Onagh, Queen 375
Oon 364
Orang Bunyi 18
Orkney 176, 240
O'Teeveth, Davie 136
Otteermaaner 122
Outhwaite, Ida Rentoul *96*

P

Paget, Walter *358*
Painajainen 230
palaces, underground 36, 38-9
Pan 18
Paracelsus 12, 34
Paterson, Cora E.M. *121*, *131*
Paton, Joseph Noel 53, *114-15*
Patrick, St 135
peapods, travelling in *118-19*
Peg Leg Jack 74
Perie 130
Pernod, Henri-Louis 233
Perrault, Charles 184
Peter Pan *59*, 407
Philomen and Baucis 344
phosphorescence 34, 92
photographs *396*, 397-9
Pilliwiggins 360
pinching 224
pine *348*, 349
Pine Tree Mary 349
Pisgies 90
Pixies *95*, 198, 364
Planck, Willy *217*
Plumstead, Joyce *77*, *196*, *201*
Polynesia 131

Ponaturi 92
pond sprites 21
Pope, Alexander 84
portals to fairy worlds 46-63
Portugal 21
Presley, Priscilla 318
primroses 360, *361*
Princess Mary's Gift Book 399, *401*
Puck *14*, *192-3*, *195*, *202*, 203-4, 268, *306-7*
punching 224

Q
Qur'an 34, 317

R
Rackham, Arthur *59*, *67*, *113*, *192-3*, *195*, *239*, *305*, *331*, *336*, *344*, *347*, *348*, *380*
Rajasthan 314
Ralston, W.R.S. 15
rath 36, 38
Ravenscroft, Thomas 238
red color 97
Redcap 97
Rhys, John 38
ring forts 36
river sprites 21
Robin Goodfellow *see* Puck
Robinson, Charles *43*
Roman mythology 291
Rossetti, Christina 211, 212
rowan 338, *339*
Rowlands, Constance E. 155
rue 354, *355*
Rumpelstiltzkin 160, 161,

162-3, 274, *275*, 276, *292-3*
Rusalka 21, 28, 56, 248
Rusal'naia nedelia 28
Russia 12, 21, 28, 76, 171, 172, 178, 198, 230, 248, 342

S
Sackville, lady Margaret *343*
Saeve *377*
saffron 130
St Agnes Eve 283
St John's Day 357
St John's Wort 357
Salvani 98
Sand Yan y Tad 34
Sandman *296*, 297
Santa Claus 6, 142
Scandinavia 36, 68, 71, 76, 160, 198, 204, 227
sceach 337
scent, floral 89
Schnezler, August 159
Scotland 36, 48, 68, 74, 78, 89, 97, 98, 102, 126, 130, 135, 172, 212, 248, 249, 342
scrying 282-3
sea 21
sea nymphs 21, *29*
seal woman 28
seduction 18
seductive spirits 208-14
Selkies 28, 82, 212
Shakespeare, William 62, 150
  Comedy of Errors 101
  Midsummer Night's Dream 66, *112*, *113*, *114-15*, *137*, *192-3*, 194, *195*,

202, 203, 251, 271, 272, *279*, 303, *304*, 305, 359, 360, 384
  Romeo and Juliet 66, 116
  Tempest 209, *239*
shaman 12
shamrock 357
shape-shifting 18, 68, 76, 197, 204, 251
Shellycoat 98
Shepherd of Myddvai 378
Shepperson, Claude *401*
Shetland Selkie 28, 82
Shining Ones 92
ships, in sky *123*
shoreline *20*
sidh (ring fort) 36
Sidhe 68, 98
Sikes, Wirt 39, 169, 366-7
Sili go Dwt 277-9
silver 382, 383
sirens 21, 28, *100*, 101, 102
siths 35
Sjörå 21
Skeaghshee 333
skin, shedding 82-3
Skogsrå 18, 19, 33, 76, 349
Slavonia 33
sleep 290
sleep disorders 230
Sleeping Beauty 216
smells 89
Snow White (Snowdrop) 156, *157*
snow-maiden 33
snowdrops 364
songs 101, 102
  of doom 102
souls 71, 90, 291
South Africa 78, 101
Spain 33, 170-1, 199

spinning 160-1, 164
spirit laughter 102
Spiritualism 89
spontaneous ignition 34
sprites:
mischief-making 197-9
water *20*, 21-31, 122
standing stones 6
steel 382
Stephens, James 54, 376, *377*
Stevenson, Robert Louis 191, 366-7
Stewart, W. Grant 229
stitchwort 356
stone monuments 36
studious spirits 35
succubus 230
Sullivan, William Holmes *50-1*
sunlight 112
swastika 387
Sweden 18, 21, 33, 34, 76, 102, 178, 249
Switzerland 265
sylphs 34

T

Tallemaja 349
Tam Lin 273, 388-9
Tarrant, Margaret W. *69*
Temme, J.D.H. 300
Ten-gu 86
Tenggren, Gustaf *168*
Tennyson, Alfred, Lord 25-6
Teutonic myths 33, 41, 71, 98, 160, 230, 297
Thailand 314
thieving 220-3
thirteenth fairy 216-19, *217*

Thomas, W. Jenkyn 277-9, 391
thorn 333, *336*, 337
Thurman, Paul *137*
thyme 356, 359
time fairies 154
Tinkerbell 407
Titania *67*, *113*, *114-15*, *137*, *304*, *305*, *306-7*, *358*
toadstools *242-3*, *244*, *245*
Tokolosh 78
Tolkien, J.R. 41, 369
Tom Thumbs 357
Tom Tit Tot 276
Tommy-Knocker 158
Tomte 178
tooth fairy 6, 318, 320-1
touching wood 332
transformations 248-55
see also shape-shifting
transitional times 290-5
transport 116-26, *117*, *118-21*, *123*, *127*
Trasgues 199
treasure 36, 41
tree spirits 86
tree-dressing *352*, 353
trees 329-53, 366-8
triskel 387
trolls 72, 78, *80-1*, 227, 276, 312, 390, 391
Tuatha dé Danaan 36, 125, 379
Turkmenistan 315
Tylwyth Teg 68

U

underground realms 36, *37*, 38-9
Underjordiske 36

V

Valkyries 33, *325*
vengeful fairies 216-19
Ventolines 33
Vily 33
vocal power 101-2
voice people 18
vulnerable moments 290-5

W

Wales 48, 68, 78, 101, 102, 126, 130, 135, 265, 266-7, 277-9, 315, 391
wands 280, *281*, 282-3
water fairies, Breton *79*
water spirits 102
water sprites *20*, 21-31, 122
Water-horses 126
weddings *322*, 323
West Africa 382
white color 98
Wicca 282
Wilde, Lady 124-5, 146, 147-9, 154, 241, 309, 330, 412
Wilde, Oscar 233
Wilde, Sir William 309
Will o' the Wisp 34
Williamson, Doris *155*
willow 350, *351*
wind, riding on 122
wind spirits 33
wings 34, 84-90, *85*, *88*, *91*
auric 89
Wolkenthrut 33
women, enticing from homes *374*, 375
Wood, Thomas 134

wood nymphs 98
wood sorrel 356
Wood-wives 19, 76, 98,
    212, 282, 333
woodland 42
Wordsworth, William 334
working attire 99
wormwood 354-6
Wright, Elsie *396*, 398-9

Y
yarrow 356
Yeats, W.B. 35, 60, 68,
    107, 190, 400
Yggdrasil *340*, 341
Yuki-Onna 33
Yunwi Djunsti 390

Z
Zaire 18
Zanzibar 86
Zieu, E. *79*

Acknowledgments

Thanks to Yvonne Deutch at MQP for kickstarting the process and being so enwrapped. To Fairy Sparkle (Rain) for parties and puppets in the woods and Lou Gray for her fairy fortieth and peg fairies. To Mike Gavin for musings on fairy folk music, Jo March and The Doc on fairy painting, Pam Verran on fairy costume. Also Jackie Owen for books and Cornish thoughts. Not least, thanks to Mrs Doonan for introducing me to Angela Carter and Alan Garner at school, and for giving us protective shells before exams.

Thanks to Brown Owl of the 1st Burley-in-Wharfedale Brownies, Yorkshire, England for their telling of the Brownie story.

Theosophical Society Book Department for extract from *Fairies: A Book of Real Fairies,* Edward L. Gardner, 1974

First published by MQ Publications Limited

12 The Ivories

6–8 Northampton Street

London, N1 2HY

email: mqpublications.com

website: www.mqpublications.com

Copyright © 2006 MQ Publications Limited

Text copyright © 2006 Susannah Marriott

ISBN (10)   1-84601-109-4

ISBN (13)   978-1-84601-109-2

10 9 8 7 6 5 4 3 2 1

Printed and bound in China